Understanding

Personality Disorder

A Guide to Help you learn about the Knowledge of the Causes, Meaning, Implications of BPD, and How to Improve Relationships Keeping Anxiety Down with Bonus Meditation

By

Peter Glisson

Contents

Introduction 10

Chapter 1: About Borderline Personality Disorder 12

1.1 What is BPD? 12

1.2 Causes of BPD 13

1.3 Symptoms of BPD 17

1.4 When to see a doctor? 20

1.5 Complications 22

1.6 Living with BPD 23

1.7 The Dark Side of Borderline Personality Disorder 24

1.8 Your Physical Health and BPD 25

1.9 Myths about BPD 26

1.10 Comparison between BPD and Other Disorders . 28

Chapter 2: Development and course of BPD 37

2.1 Early Onset in Adolescence 37

2.2 Risk for development of BPD symptoms 38

2.3 BPD in adulthood 40

2.4 Factors for recovery 42

Chapter 3: Emotion Regulation in Borderline Personality Disorder 46

3.1 What Is Emotion Regulation? 46

3.2 Emotion Regulation vs. Dysregulation 47

3.3 BPD and Emotional Issues 48

3.4 Difficulty in Controlling Anger 49

3.5 Fear of Abandonment and Paranoia 50

3.6 Irritability and Rapid Mood Swings *50*

3.7 Consistent Feelings of Emptiness *51*

3.8 Managing Emotions Despite BPD *52*

Chapter 4: Struggles in Relationships **54**

4.1 Struggles Families of BPD Patients Experience *56*

4.2 Stress on the Family *57*

4.3 Responsibility and Guilt *58*

4.4 Getting Help *59*

4.5 Broader Effects *60*

4.6 Making a relationship work when one of you has BPD *61*

4.7 What if you are in a relationship with someone with BPD? *62*

4.8 Relationships over social media *63*

4.9 What if a patient with BPD has kids? *65*

4.10 Outlook for relationship *65*

4.11 What does it take to feel better? *66*

4.12 borderline personality disorder during pregnancy *66*

Chapter 5: How to improve social relations? **68**

5.1 What you need to know about BPD! *69*

5.2 Learning all you can *70*

5.3 Recognizing the symptoms and signs of BPD *71*

5.4 Things People with Borderline Personality Disorder Want You to Know *73*

5.5 If You Want to Help Someone with BPD, First, You Have to Take Care of Yourself *80*

5.6 Remember the 3 C's rule............................. 82

5.7 How to communicate with someone who has BPD
.... 83

5.8 Communication tips 84

5.9 How to set and reinforce healthy boundaries? 86

5.10 Setting healthy boundaries with a borderline loved one 88

5.11 Supporting your loved one's BPD treatment........ 89

5.12 How to support treatment?........................... 90

5.13 Setting goals for BPD recovery - Go slowly........... 91

Chapter 6: Workplace and BPD 92

6.1 Working with BPD.. 92

6.2 Effects of Symptoms and Signs of BPD at Work...... 94

6.3 Finding the Best Job for You.......................... 95

6.4 Get to Know Yourself 96

6.5 How to Cope with BPD in the Workplace.............. 97

6.6 Building a Strong Career 98

6.7 Some Tips for Working Excellently with BPD 99

6.8 Helping an employee with BPD............................ 103

6.9 Some Tips for Working with Clients with Borderline Personality Disorder.. 105

6.10 Accommodations for employees with BPD........ 110

**Chapter 7: Understanding Stigma When You Have BPD
.... 113**

7.1 The Stigma of Mental Illness 114

7.2 The Stigma Associated with Borderline Personality Disorder 115

7.3 Stigma's Impact on Treatment............................ 116

7.4 Manifestations of Borderline Personality Disorder Stigma 117

7.5 The Damage of Stigma 119

7.6 Breaking Through Prejudice to Find Healing 121

Chapter 8: Bonus Meditation............................ **124**

8.1 How to Practice Music Meditation?.................... 124

8.2 How Mindfulness Meditation Can Help Borderline Personality Disorder... 127

8.3 Religious or Spiritual Meditation........................ 130

8.4 Traditional Meditation.................................... 134

Chapter 9: Some Strategies for Supporting Someone with BPD **136**

9.1. Learn about BPD. 137

9.2. Show confidence and respect.......................... 138

9.3. Be trustworthy. 138

9.4 Manage conflict with attachment. 139

9.5 Encourage Professional Help. 140

9.6. Identify strengths. 140

9.7. Have fun together..................................... 141

9.8. Take suicide seriously. 141

Chapter 10: Splitting in Borderline Personality Disorder 143

10.1 What is splitting in BPD? 144

10.2 How long does splitting last?......................... 145

10.3 What can cause a splitting episode? 145

10.4 Examples of splitting.................................. 146

10.5 How does splitting affect relationships? 148

10.6 What's the best way to cope with splitting if you have BPD? 149

10.7 What's the best way to help a person who's experiencing splitting?..................................... 150

Chapter 11: Treatments and Therapies.......................... 151

11.1 Goals of treatment................................... 151

11.2 When should treatment start? 152

11.3 Tests and Diagnosis 152

11.4 One major challenge: finding effective treatment 153

11.5 Seek and Stick with Treatment.................... 154

11.6 Care program approach (CPA)..................... 156

11.7 Psychotherapy... 156

11.8 Dialectical behavior therapy (DBT) 157

11.9 Mentalization-based therapy (MBT)............... 159

11.10 Therapeutic communities (TCs) 161

11.11 Cognitive Behavioral Therapy (CBT) 163

11.12 Transference-Focused Therapy (TFT) 165

11.13 Arts therapies....................................... 167

11.14 Treating a crisis 168

11.15 Hospitalization...................................... 170

11.16 Medications.. 170

11.17 Alternative therapy................................. 172

11.18 Tips for Getting the Most Out of BPD Treatment 172

11.19 Overcoming BPD Without Medication............ 173

Chapter 12: Other Elements of Care............................ **175**

12.1 How to try to keep anxiety down at all times 175

12.2 Therapy for Caregivers and Family Members.... 184

12.3 Tips for Family and Caregivers............................ 185

12.4 Coping Skills for Borderline Personality Disorder. 186

12.5 What if the person doesn't want help?.............. 191

Chapter 13: 7 Stages of Healing of Individuals with Borderline Personality Disorder **192**

13.1 Denial. 193

13.2 Confusion. 194

13.3 Resistance. 195

13.4 Anger. 195

13.5 Depression. 196

13.6 Acceptance. 197

13.7 Therapy. 198

Conclusion **200**

Introduction

A borderline personality disorder is a psychological disorder that affects how you think and feels about others and yourself, making it difficult to function in daily life. Self-esteem problems, trouble regulating emotions and behavior, and history of insecure relationships are all part of it.

You may have a strong fear of abandonment or insecurity if you have borderline personality disorder, and you may find it difficult to tolerate being alone. Even if you desire to have meaningful and enduring relationships, improper anger, impulsiveness, and frequent mood swings may drive people away.

By early adulthood, most people have developed borderline personality disorder. The disease seems to be worsening in early adulthood and may improve with age.

It is estimated that 1.6 percent of the adult population in the United States suffers from BPD. Women account for almost seventy-five percent of those diagnosed with BPD. A recent study indicates that males are just as susceptible to BPD as women but are more often misdiagnosed with depression or PTSD.

Don't give up if you have borderline personality disorder. Many individuals with this condition improve with therapy over time and may learn to live happy lives.

One of the most harmful misunderstandings about BPD is that it is a life sentence, that individuals with the illness will suffer from it for the rest of their lives and that there is nothing that can be done to help them. The phrase "personality disorder" does not help matters since it suggests something fundamentally wrong with a person's personality.

In fact, there are many reasons to be optimistic. To begin with, research has shown that recovery rates from BPD are considerably greater than previously believed.

For at least four years, 86 percent of individuals with BPD stopped fulfilling BPD criteria, and 50 percent of people recovered entirely (no longer fulfilling the BPD criteria and having good work and social functioning)

Many of these individuals were getting therapy, while others were not. Despite the fact that many individuals with BPD obviously suffer for a long time, BPD is not an incurable illness, and many people recover.

Chapter 1: About Borderline Personality Disorder

1.1   What is BPD?

Borderline personality disorder (BPD) is a mental illness. Because of its historical significance, the term "borderline" is included in the name of this disease. In the past, mental disorders were classified as either 'neuroses' or 'psychoses', respectively. Back in the day, when psychiatrists initially described BPD, it didn't fall into either group. They came to the conclusion that it belonged on an arbitrary line between these two types of diseases. It appears during adolescence or the early stages of adulthood. Emotional instability, a distorted self-image, impulsive behavior, and unstable relationships are all symptoms. According to the National Institute of Mental Health, BPD affects approximately 1.6 percent of people in the United States.

1.2   Causes of BPD

Borderline personality disorder has no one cause, and a combination of causes most likely causes it.

Genetics

You may be more prone to developing BPD if you inherit genes from your parents.

According to one research, if one identical twin has BPD, the second identical twin has a 2-in-3 probability of having BPD.

These results should be interpreted with care since there is no evidence of a gene for BPD.

Biological Factors

According to many studies, people with BPD have variations in both the structure and function of their brains. Excessive activity in regions of the brain that regulate emotion experience and expression has been linked to BPD.

Individuals with BPD, for example, exhibit higher levels of activation in the limbic system, which regulates fear, anger, and aggressiveness, than people without BPD. This may be linked to BPD's emotional instability symptoms. Newer research has shown links between the hormone oxytocin and the development of BPD.

Abuse and trauma: BPD are more common in those who have been emotionally, sexually, or physically abused. Neglect, mistreatment, or being separated from a parent are all factors that increase the risk.

Problem with brain chemicals

Many individuals with BPD are believed to have a problem with the neurotransmitters in brain, especially the serotonin. Imbalances of serotonin have been related to depression, aggressiveness, and the inability to control harmful urges.

These neurotransmitters are some chemicals that act as messengers and that your brain uses to communicate with other brain cells.

Problem with brain development

The brains of individuals with BPD have been studied using MRI. Strong magnetic fields and radio waves are used in

MRI scans to provide a detailed picture of the body's interior.

The scans showed that three brain regions in many individuals with BPD were either smaller than anticipated or had very high levels of activity. These were the components:

- The amygdala is involved in regulating emotions, particularly "negative" emotions like fear, aggressiveness, and anxiety.

- The orbitofrontal cortex – which is involved in decision making and planning

- The hippocampus – which helps in regulating self-control and behavior

Problems with these areas of the brain may have a role in BPD symptoms.

Your early upbringing has an impact on the development of various regions of the brain. These areas of the brain are also in charge of mood regulation, which may explain some of the difficulties that individuals with BPD experience in intimate relationships.

Environmental factors

Among individuals with BPD, a variety of environmental variables seem to be frequent and widespread. Being a victim of physical, emotional, or sexual abuse is one of them.

Growing up with another family member who had a severe mental health issue, such as bipolar disorder or a drink or drug abuse problem, being exposed to long-term anxiety or anguish as a kid being mistreated by one or both parents

The way people view the world and what they think about other people is heavily influenced by their connection with their parents and relatives.

Unresolved childhood fear, anger, and grief may lead to a range of flawed adult thinking patterns, such as expecting others to be your parent, expecting other people to bully you, idealizing others, and acting as if other people are adults while you aren't.

1.3 Symptoms of BPD

Signs of borderline personality disorder

How you feel about yourself, how you interact with others, and how you act are all affected by borderline personality disorder.

Signs and symptoms may include:

- A strong fear of abandonment, to the point of going to extremes to escape separation or rejection, whether actual or imagined.

- A pattern of insecure, intense interactions, such as idealizing someone one minute and then thinking that person doesn't love enough or is unkind the next.

- Rapid shifts in self-identity and self-image, such as changing objectives and values and perceiving oneself as terrible or non-existent.

- Stress-related paranoia and a loss of contact with reality may last anywhere from a few minutes to many hours.

- Gambling, unsafe sex, reckless driving, spending sprees, drug abuse, binge eating, or sabotaging success by abruptly leaving a good job or terminating a great relationship are examples of impulsive and risky behavior.

- Suicidal threats or conduct and self-injury are common responses to the fear of rejection or separation.

- Wide mood fluctuations may last anywhere between a few hours to a few days and include extreme happiness, anger, embarrassment, and anxiety.

- Feelings of emptiness that persist.

- Anger that is inappropriate or excessive, such as losing your temper often, being sarcastic or bitter, or getting into physical fights.

Emotional symptoms

The inability to control one's emotions is a common sign of BPD. The individual may experience strong emotions for extended periods and returning to a baseline emotion after enduring emotional stress may be more challenging.

The individual may also have strong emotions of rage or have trouble managing their anger. This is often followed by feelings of shame or guilt, which may negatively impact a person's self-esteem. This rage is often fueled by a fear of neglect, indifference, or abandonment.

Another frequent symptom is self-harm. People with BPD may use this to regulate their emotions, punish themselves, or communicate their inner anguish.

Recurrent suicidal thoughts are another sign of BPD. Certain individuals also make suicide attempts. Self-harm and suicide are more common in individuals with BPD than in those without.

Effective therapy may assist individuals in managing their emotions and reducing the frequency or severity of self-harm and suicidal thoughts.

Relationship difficulties

Patterns of unstable or intense relationships are common among people with BPD. A change from intense admiration to extreme hate, often known as a shift from idealization to devaluation, may be involved.

Attempts to prevent actual or perceived abandonment may characterize relationships. The fear of being abandoned may negatively affect a person's self-esteem, emotions, thoughts, and actions.

For example, the individual may get panicked or enraged when separated from people they care about.

1.4   When to see a doctor?

If you see any of the signs or symptoms listed above, speak with your doctor or mental health professional.

If you have suicidal thoughts

If you are having suicidal thoughts or dreams about harming yourself, seek assistance right immediately by doing one of the following things:

- Immediately dial 911 or your local emergency number.

- Make a call to a suicide prevention hotline. Call the National Suicide Prevention Lifeline at 1-800-273-TALK (1-800-273-8255) anytime in the United States. To contact the Veterans Crisis Line, dial the same number and press "1."

- Contact a mental health professional, a doctor, or another health care professional.

- Make contact with a family member, close friend, trustworthy peer, or coworker.

- Make contact with a member of your faith community.

- Talk to a family member or acquaintance about visiting a medical or mental health professional if you see signs or symptoms in them. However, you cannot make someone seek assistance. If the relationship is causing you a lot of stress, you may choose to visit a therapist on your own.

1.5 Complications

Many aspects of your life may be affected by borderline personality disorder. It may have a detrimental impact on personal relationships, work, education, social activities, and self-esteem, leading to:

- Job losses or changes frequently.

- Failure to complete a degree course.

- There are a variety of legal concerns, including the possibility of prison time.

- Turbulent relationships, marital stress, or divorce are all possibilities.

- Self-injury, such as slashing or burning oneself, and hospitalization regularly.

- Participation in abusive relationships.

- Due to impulsive and hazardous conduct, there can be sexually transmitted diseases, unplanned pregnancies, car accidents, and physical fights.

- Suicide attempts.

- You may also be suffering from other mental health issues, such as depression.

- Misuse of alcohol or other substances.

- Misuse of alcohol or other substances.

- Anxiety disorders.

- Bipolar disorder.

- Attention deficit hyperactivity disorder (ADHD).

- Post-traumatic stress disorder (PTSD).

- Other types of personality disorders.

1.6 Living with BPD

Everyday occurrences may trigger these symptoms. Adolescents and teenagers with BPD, for example, may get enraged and upset when they are separated from individuals they care about, such as during vacations, travels, or unexpected changes in plans. According to research, young individuals with this condition may perceive anger in an emotionally neutral face and respond more strongly to words with negative associations than those without the disorder.

This unpredictable oscillation makes BPD so difficult to explain, especially to people who are close to you. It is best treated with patience and understanding, as is the case with other mental illnesses. And, like depression or hypomania, it puts the burden of caring on others who aren't always in a position to understand or help, no matter how much they care about you. BPD may make both partners feel isolated in a relationship.

1.7 The Dark Side of Borderline Personality Disorder

Living with or being with someone who has this personality disorder may be very challenging. It brings out one's ruthless side in a shocking way. BPD is like a Terminator vision that exposes the chinks in everyone's armor.

The major risk to the human body is the human mind. Borderline Personality Disorder is a mental illness that affects over 10% of the population yet remains a confusing enigma to this day. Fatalities of this deadly illness are often trapped within their impulsivity, unable to break free from their destructive cycles of self-blame and manipulation. Victims on the border may be dangerous.

They stay, imprisoned, within their rash and neurotic brains of self-mutilation, constant accusations, and vicious manipulations in the pursuit of unknown desires. Borderline people are among the most turbulent in love relationships, enticing their partners before displaying callous indifference and infatuated terrorizations resulting from contradictory emotions. When the world fails to match with borderline patients' extreme ideals, high levels of impulsivity cause them to indulge in physical and emotional self-injurious activities. The human race is trapped in the emotional mind forever. Rather than our logical and reasonable thinking, emotions dictate our daily judgments and actions, acting on a lack of inhibitions and suppressed traumatic suffering despite awareness. Humanity has been affected by societal pressure to suppress raw emotions to achieve the appearance of acceptance by becoming exact replicas of others, imprisoning passions and feelings waiting to be released, and locking our individualities within our minds.

1.8 Your Physical Health and BPD

Unfortunately, borderline personality disorder (BPD) may have a negative effect on your physical health as well. In addition to chronic pain, chronic fatigue syndrome and fibromyalgia, arthritis, diabetes, obesity, and other severe health issues are linked with bipolar disorder (BPD). BPD is also linked with unhealthy lifestyle choices such as smoking, excessive alcohol use, and a lack of regular physical activity.

1.9 Myths about BPD

Some mental health professionals, as well as the general public, are misinformed about this illness. This ambiguity may have an effect on and affect the way that individuals are treated. Even worse, long-standing misconceptions about the illness may prevent individuals from seeking treatment for it, particularly if they believe their experience is being misinterpreted by others.

The following are some popular myths and misconceptions:

Myth: It is incurable.

Borderline personality disorder is a condition that is treatable. Historically, since BPD had an impact on someone's personality, many people were quick to infer that it was untreatable due to the fact that someone's personality cannot be changed.

Many therapies, including mentalization-based treatment (MBT), dialectical behavior therapy (DBT), and transference-focused psychotherapy, have lately been shown to be successful as treatments (TFP). General psychiatric management (GPM), a less intense strategy that is becoming more popular throughout the globe, is one of the techniques being used more often.

A BPD diagnosis does not imply that a person will be tormented by symptoms for the rest of his or her life. Symptoms fluctuate in intensity and frequency as a result of therapy. It is possible for many individuals who have the disease to have productive lives.

Myth: People suffering from borderline personality disorder (BPD) are victims of child abuse.

The truth is that this is not always the case.

While some instances of borderline personality disorder are caused by childhood trauma, it is more probable that a diagnosis is the consequence of a mix of contextual variables rather than one single one. Attachment, early trauma, biological variables, and social factors are all examples of risk factors.

Myth: It is just a women's disease.

It is estimated that approximately 14 million people in the United States suffer from BPD. Previously thought to be more prevalent in women, the biggest research ever conducted on mental illnesses has shown that it affects both men and women equally.

One possible reason why it seems to impact more women than men is that women are more likely than males to seek mental health treatment. Because research on borderline personality disorder is often performed in a psychiatric environment, males with borderline personality disorder were historically less likely to be included in these research initiatives.

The fact that BPD is often misdiagnosed in males is another reason. Many of the males who suffer from the disease are also diagnosed with depression or post-traumatic stress disorder (PTSD).

1.10 Comparison between BPD and Other Disorders

BPD and Narcissism:

While there are many similarities in the signs and symptoms of borderline and narcissistic personality disorders, there are also significant distinctions between the two. Even if there are significant distinctions, proper clinical diagnosis is required. However, there are certain parallels in treating the illnesses, which may involve long-term psychotherapy in a friendly residential environment.

Symptoms of Narcissism include:

- Bragging about your accomplishment's superior traits

- Lack of empathy for other people

- Insulting others or making yourself look well at the expense of other people

- Criticizing or Flattering —depending on whether others criticize or flatter in return

- Sensitivity in the face of even potential criticism

- Dominating relationships and interactions

- Needing flattery and attention

- Aloof and distant in relationships

- Fantasizing about fame, power, and wealth

- Impatience

- Moodiness

- Difficulty adapting to change

- Envy, revenge, and resentment

Insecurity is a significant problem that underpins both disorders to some extent. These anxieties are so overpowering that they distort the individual's views of himself and others, even when they are not visible on the surface. Consequently, individuals suffering from borderline personality disorder or narcissistic personality disorder are more likely than the general population to engage in patterns of unstable or harmful relationships. In both instances, the subject of abandonment is prevalent. When a person has borderline personality disorder, they may play out their strong anxieties of abandonment to the point where they push someone away from them. When it comes to abandonment, however, someone suffering from narcissistic personality disorder is more likely to be the one doing it. This may be because they would like to do it before someone else has the opportunity to forsake them or to support their image of superiority otherwise.

BPD and Bipolar Disorder

These two diseases are often mistaken for one another. They both exhibit signs of impulsiveness and mood swings, for example. However, these are two distinct disorders that need two distinct therapies. Bipolar disease, often known as manic depression, is characterized by extreme fluctuations in energy, mood, and the capacity to perform throughout the day. Bipolar disorder is a mental illness that affects the ability to function.

Symptoms of Bipolar Disorder Include:

During times of mania, the symptoms might include:

- More mental and physical energy and activity than normal
- An excessively angry, happy, or irritated mood
- Racing thoughts and ideas
- Making big plans
- Talking more and faster
- Risk taking
- Less sleep, with no feeling of tiredness
- Impulsiveness (sex, substance abuse, spending, etc.)
- Poor judgement

During times of depression, the symptoms might include:

- Lasting sadness
- Drop in energy

- Less activity and energy

- Problems making decisions and concentrating

- Irritability and restlessness

- No interest in favorite activities

- Anxiety

- Worry

- Change in sleep patterns or appetite

- Feelings of hopelessness and guilt; suicidal thoughts

Those with bipolar illness display stability that people with a borderline personality disorder do not exhibit when they are not experiencing manic or depressive episodes. The average bipolar individual can operate quite well in the world while they are between episodes. It is possible for them to have close relationships that are disrupted by their times of sickness, but when they are not having episodes, they have a level of stability that you do not see in a borderline personality.

Bipolar disorder is more deeply entrenched in the anatomy of the nervous system and is more susceptible to treatment than other types of mental illness. In addition to the science of the brain and neurological system, a borderline personality disorder is heavily influenced by the psychological level of the mind - the manner in which meaning is created. A more biological disease such as bipolar disorder does not have these deeply entrenched psychological elements or ways of viewing the world and seeing oneself and others, which are present in bipolar disorder.

Mood fluctuations associated with bipolar illness are more random and less linked to events than those associated with a borderline personality disorder. Those suffering from bipolar disorder may have a hair-trigger reaction during an episode, while those suffering from borderline personality disorder experience a hair-trigger reaction all of the time.

BPD and Complex Post-Traumatic Stress Disorder

When a terrifying incident occurs, either directly or by witnessing it, a mental health condition is known as post-traumatic stress disorder (PTSD) may develop. In addition to uncontrolled thoughts about the incident, flashbacks and nightmares are common symptoms of post-traumatic stress disorder (PTSD).

BPD is a disease that is not completely understood, and research into its causes has produced contradictory results. Some studies have shown that individuals diagnosed with BPD had a history of trauma or neglect, especially children, which suggests that the disorder may have been brought on by an environmental factor. Another study has indicated that there is a genetic connection between the two conditions based on family history.

C-PTSD is considered to be a subtype of post-traumatic stress disorder (PTSD), which is thought to develop as a result of repeated exposure to trauma. Survivors of long-term relationship violence and child abuse are more likely to be diagnosed with this condition. Children who have been subjected to abuse are especially vulnerable to developing C-PTSD since the sense of being unable to escape the abuse or of being dependent on the source of the trauma is associated with the development of the disorder.

Because of the similarities in symptoms between BPD and C-PTSD, the two conditions are frequently mistaken. Emotional discomfort is a feature of both conditions; certain events may trigger these distressing feelings. Significant responses such as dissociation, suicidal ideation, anxiety, flashbacks, and/or despair may occur as a result of these triggers. Other commonalities include low self-esteem, emotional outbursts, and difficulties in establishing and maintaining good interpersonal connections.

While individuals suffering from C-PTSD and BPD both exhibit difficulties with interpersonal skills, the underlying reasons for these difficulties are thought to be distinct. In BPD, there is usually a fear of abandonment, while this is not prevalent in traumatic brain injury (TBI). Fear manifests itself in relationships in those suffering from C-PTSD, but in a more internalized manner. Instead of being terrified of being abandoned by another person, someone suffering from C-PTSD may believe that they are unlovable or damaged. One significant distinction between these two diseases is how they respond to emotions that are similar. Self-harm is very rare in those suffering from C-PTSD, but it is much more frequent in people suffering from BPD. Yet another distinction between the two groups' responses is their readiness to participate in any kind of interpersonal interaction. A person suffering from C-PTSD is more prone to avoid relationships out of fear, while a person suffering from BPD is more likely to surround themselves with others in an effort to erase any possible emotions of abandonment or rejection.

The struggle with one's identity or one's self-concept is a frequent symptom for individuals suffering from C-PTSD as well as BPD. This, on the other hand, tends to manifest itself in a variety of ways. In contrast to individuals suffering from BPD, people suffering from C-PTSD often have severe emotions of being "damaged," which is prevalent among those suffering from shame-based mental illnesses. People who have a borderline personality disorder (BPD) have a less clear sense of who they are. In order to fit in with different social groups, it is typical for individuals to change their interests. They have also often described feeling confused or unable to figure out who they really are.

Chapter 2: Development and course of BPD

BPD may be diagnosed as early as 12 years old if symptoms persist for at least a year, according to the DSM-5. The majority of diagnoses, however, are made in early adulthood or late adolescence. Before BPD diagnosis, the most typical course of borderline personality disorder is chronic instability in years of teenage and early adulthood, with episodes of severe emotional and impulsive responses leading to the recurrent need of emergency services at every crisis. Almost 40% of individuals with BPD have been misdiagnosed with bipolar disorder in the past. Without knowledge of the BPD population in young people, adequate resources for early intervention and avoiding crystallization of behaviors that may have severe effects on functioning are unlikely to be available.

2.1 Early Onset in Adolescence

While there is not much research on BPD in kids, there is increasing evidence of BPD symptoms and characteristics manifesting throughout adolescence. As adolescents are expected to interact with the world more freely, emotional regulation and self-control issues become increasingly evident at this stage of development. Self-harm, a defining feature of BPD, has been observed in two-thirds of patients, beginning in adolescence and other impulsive and risky behaviors.

Young people with BPD symptoms are more likely to have weak functioning as adults, including poor academic, social, and occupational outcomes since BPD symptoms cause more developmental processes. Even though they no longer meet the official diagnosis criteria, many individuals maintain residual BPD symptoms later in life. On the other hand, BPD characteristics are unstable throughout adolescence and therefore do not constitute a lifelong disorder.

2.2 Risk for development of BPD symptoms

Although the exact origin of borderline personality disorder is unknown, research indicates that brain structure, genetics, function, cultural, environmental, and social factors all have a role or may increase the chance of having the disorder.

Parental mental disorder

A parent with a history of any mental illness puts their kid at risk for mental illness due to genetic and environmental factors. According to studies, first-degree relatives of people with BPD are 4 to 20 times more likely to develop BPD than the general population. Because BPD has many traits with other mental illnesses, it is no surprise that relatives of people with BPD are more likely to develop substance use disorders, depression, and antisocial personality disorder.

Family environment

When a kid's neurological vulnerabilities are combined with an invalidating environment, the child is more likely to develop BPD as an adult. Low family unity, high levels of mother-child discord, and low maternal support may be invalidating environments.

Substance use disorder, depression, and suicidal behaviors

Early start of psychiatric diagnoses, such as depression and drug use disorder, puts young people at risk for academic and interpersonal impairments and disrupts normal development for everyday functioning, which may lead to the appearance of personality disorder later in life. The most frequent cause of adolescent suicide is separation at a young age and interpersonal conflict.

Cultural, Environmental, and Social Factors. Many individuals with borderline personality disorder report having been experienced terrible life experiences as children, such as abuse, abandonment, or hardship. Others may have been exposed to invalidating or unstable relationships as well as hostile conflict.

Although these variables may raise a person's chance of developing a borderline personality disorder, it does not guarantee that they will develop the disorder. Similarly, there can be individuals without these risk factors who may acquire borderline personality disorder at some point in their lives.

2.3 BPD in adulthood

Because most BPD diagnoses are not made until a person reaches 18, therapy typically starts in adulthood. According to studies, the majority of individuals with BPD improve with time. After two years, one-fourth of patients have a remission (less than two symptoms for two months or longer) from their BPD diagnosis. After ten years, 85 percent achieving remission 12 months or more, and 91 percent of patients were in remission for at least two months. As a result, BPD has a typically favorable outcome.

When looking at the progression of specific BPD symptoms, most studies show an overall decrease in all symptoms, with impulsive and behavioral manifestations of BPD resolving faster than emotional affective experiences. Although self-harm and suicidal behavior are reduced early on, the risk of total suicide remains around 10% when patients are in their 30s and have tried several therapies. BPD has a greater overall mortality rate than the general population.

Other mental illnesses, such as mood disorders, anxiety disorders, substance use disorders, and eating disorders, are very prevalent in people with BPD symptoms. Even after a 6-year follow-up, more than 60% of BPD patients met the criterion for a mood disorder, and a comparable percentage fulfilled the criteria for anxiety disorder. BPD diagnosis is also related to a prolonged recovery period for other mental illnesses and medical problems. During the 8-year follow-up, medical and psychiatric medication usage decreases, but after that, it remains essentially constant.

Most specialized BPD therapies are now restricted to 1 to 3 years and are costly. Some specialists believe that an intermittent psychotherapy approach would be more effective in treating the many issues that arise at different phases of life in people with a wide range of BPD characteristics. Dialectical Behavior Therapy, for example, was created to treat self-harm and suicidal behavior, which are prevalent in the early stages of BPD but go away with time. As a result, learning to handle feelings of emptiness and fear of abandonment using a therapy method that is most helpful for the specified symptom may be more relevant to older patients.

2.4 Factors for recovery

Remission from symptoms coupled with excellent, full-time vocational or educational functioning and at least one supportive and stable connection with a friend or partner constitutes recovery from BPD. Not being hospitalized, a higher IQ, previous excellent occupational performance, high agreeableness, high extraversion, and the absence of dependent, avoidant, and obsessive-compulsive personality disorders are all predictors of recovery. Marriage and becoming a parent at an older age than non-recovered people with BPD are also related to successful treatment.

Suppose you or someone you care about has been diagnosed with borderline personality disorder (BPD). In that case, your first inquiry will almost certainly be whether or not the illness can be rectified or treated. While there is no definite cure for borderline personality disorder, it is completely curable. As a matter of fact, with the appropriate treatment strategy, you may be well on your way to recovery and remission.

While remission and recovery may not always imply a "cure," they do represent a successful therapy for borderline personality disorder.

As defined by the BPD Association, remission is the stage in which you no longer fulfill the stated criteria for being diagnosed with BPD.

Recovery is a less well-defined term, but it implies that you are able to operate in all areas of your life for a long period of time after an illness or injury. This involves holding onto a job and maintaining important interpersonal connections, among other things.

According to research published in 2015, the vast majority of individuals who suffer from BPD will no longer satisfy the diagnostic criteria for the illness by the time they reach the age of majority. According to all accounts, the majority of individuals ultimately outgrow their symptoms and attain remission as a result of the disease's natural course.

Research published in 2012 monitored 290 individuals with (BPD) every two years for a total of sixteen years. What they discovered was that remission (defined as no longer fulfilling the diagnostic criteria for at least two years) was more likely to occur spontaneously within two to eight years after the initial diagnosis and therapy than they had anticipated.

After 16 years, 99 percent of the patients had obtained a two-year remission, with 78 percent having attained an eight-year remission throughout that time. The same research discovered that symptom relapses tended to diminish with time as well, with a peak of 36 percent after two years and a low of approximately 10 percent after eight years after treatment began.

To be clear, these data are based on individuals who have been diagnosed with and treated for borderline personality disorder (BPD). The findings did not contain information on the kinds of therapy given or whether or not maintenance treatments were used. Therefore, it is unclear how much the different therapies affected remission rates or whether individuals who have not been diagnosed would outgrow the disease as a result of the treatments.

Chapter 3: Emotion Regulation in Borderline Personality Disorder

Many individuals who have borderline personality disorder (BPD) have difficulty controlling their emotions. Emotional dysregulation is a key symptom of BPD, and it may explain other symptoms such as risky or impulsive behavior, unstable relationships, and stress-related cognitive abnormalities. Emotional instability is also a criterion for diagnosing BPD.

3.1 What Is Emotion Regulation?

Emotion regulation refers to a person's ability to connect to and act on emotional events in various ways. This involves the capacity to:

- This involves the capacity to:

- Recognize, comprehend, and accept your emotional experiences.

- To deal with unpleasant emotions, use appropriate coping mechanisms.

During times of emotional stress, people with emotion management abilities can resist the impulses to engage in impulsive actions such as self-harm, reckless conduct, or physical violence.

During childhood, children's emotional control abilities develop. We acquire techniques as we become older to help us comprehend what we are experiencing and self-soothe when we are upset. Several factors may sabotage this process, including:

- Trauma or stress in childhood.

- Parents who are harsh or dominating.

- Differences in the structure of the brain.

- Lack of a solid connection with one's parents.

3.2 Emotion Regulation vs. Dysregulation

While emotion regulation helps us deal with setbacks, someone who suffers from emotion dysregulation will have difficulty understanding and healthily reacting to their emotions. This is particularly important in BPD since individuals with the disorder often feel considerable discomfort in emotional circumstances.

Our ability to regulate our emotions significantly impacts how we react to situations in our lives. When someone with emotion management abilities, for example, has a breakup, they will certainly feel sad and even depressed, but they will be able to regulate their feelings and continue with their regular activities.

If someone with BPD is exposed to the same scenario, they may get depressed to the point of being unable to function. They may cope by indulging in self-destructive or aggressive conduct, as well as impulsive behaviors such as promiscuity.

3.3 BPD and Emotional Issues

People with BPD have a variety of symptoms that are linked to their capacity to control their emotions. These may cause major difficulties in everyday life by creating anxiety and despair, making it difficult to establish solid relationships, or causing workplace challenges.

As a method to deal with emotion dysregulation, people with BPD may engage in impulsive, self-destructive, or even self-harming behaviors.

Contact the National Suicide Prevention Lifeline at 1-800-273-8255 for support and guidance from a professional counselor if you are experiencing suicidal thoughts. Call 911 if you or a loved one is in immediate danger.

3.4 Difficulty in Controlling Anger

Severe anger appears out of nowhere, along with intense mood swings. Even little irritations may cause anger in people with BPD, leading to destructive or violent actions such as self-harm.

Anger control issues seem to be strongly related to emotional dysregulation. Relationship intensity and stability may also have a role, as individuals in unstable, chaotic relationships are more likely to act aggressively.

3.5 Fear of Abandonment and Paranoia

BPD patients often fear being rejected, alone, or abandoned by people closest to them, leading to paranoia. This may cause them to behave obsessively, continuously seeking reassurance, or even drive people away to prevent being hurt by future rejection. Many of these habits, however, may contribute to a lack of solid relationships.

This may be made worse by a lack of emotional regulation. Intense emotional outbursts may drive people away, and an inability to calm paranoia or insecurity may lead to additional marital instability.

3.6 Irritability and Rapid Mood Swings

Borderline personality disorder causes anxiety and irritation because people with the condition have difficulty controlling their moods and expressing their feelings. Mood swings may be both strong and fast.

These worry and irritation emotions may interfere with your usual tasks, such as working or caring for yourself. Others may find it difficult to be around you during these periods for various reasons, causing your relationships to suffer.

The mood swings and anger that individuals with BPD experience may be due to emotional sensitivity. Someone with this disease is more likely to be emotionally sensitive in general, leading them to respond to events rapidly and strongly.

3.7 Consistent Feelings of Emptiness

BPD patients often report a persistent sense of emptiness. While the source of this sensation is unknown, it may be linked to a negative self-image. Someone with BPD may find it difficult to maintain a strong sense of self and feel detached from themselves and others.

This sense of emptiness is very disruptive, leading to rash decisions, self-harm, and suicide.

It may also lead to loneliness since someone who suffers from chronic emptiness may feel cut off from others and find it difficult to sustain friendships. If you are feeling lonely, it may be difficult to control your emotions, leading to a vicious cycle that exacerbates your feelings of sadness and emptiness.

3.8 Managing Emotions Despite BPD

If you are having trouble with BPD and emotion control, you should consult a therapist specializing in this area. They'll have a better grasp of what's causing your emotional problems, and you'll be able to work together on methods to help you learn to control your emotions and manage mood swings.

People with BPD have found that dialectical behavior treatment (DBT) is especially beneficial.

This kind of treatment was created specially to assist individuals with BPD in learning how to change their beliefs and actions, thus decreasing the condition's symptoms.

Apart from treatment, there are several self-help methods for BPD that may help you better control your emotions.

Some of these are:

- When you are in a bad mood, use grounding methods.

- Exercising regularly.

- Writing is a great way to express your feelings.

- Mindfulness meditation is being practiced.

- Educating oneself more about BPD.

- Incorporating stress-reduction methods into your life.

Chapter 4: Struggles in Relationships

Young individuals with BPD tend to change professions often and suddenly cut connections with people they care about due to their impulsiveness. They also experience many strong and abrupt mood swings, and we have a lot of trouble controlling their emotions. When they make a mistake, they unintentionally blame others, which leads them to be manipulative and harsh to people they care about.

Borderline personality disorder (BPD) is a debilitating mental illness that affects more than just the individual who has it. It affects everyone they have a connection with, including their family, friends, and partners or spouses.

The whole family of a person with borderline personality may suffer because of the numerous family problems directly affected by borderline personality behaviors and symptoms.

These are some of the most frequent family consequences of BPD, as well as where you may get help as a family.

Mental disorders have an impact on the whole family. Due to the inherent problems in interpersonal interactions, this impact is particularly severe in personality disorders. In the lives of individuals with borderline personality disorder, family members are usually the most impacted (BPD). As a result, they affect the person who is suffering from the condition.

When a loved one suffers a crisis, family members, typically parents or spouses, must often take control, which sometimes necessitates brief psychiatric hospitalizations or visits to the emergency room. Family members must deal with suicidal behavior.

Close family members frequently take the burden of a sick person's mood swings and outbursts of wrath directed at those closest to them.

Family members may perceive the sick individual as trying to burn bridges with helpful resources. People with BPD risk having those who have been helpful, caring, and protective abandon them, leaving them to fend for themselves in the world. As a result, they are afraid of being abandoned. Relapse is their reaction to fear. They may not want to relapse on purpose, but fear and worry may lead them to revert to old coping mechanisms.

When witnessing a loved one with BPD engage in self-destructive behaviors, family members frequently feel powerless. This is especially true for parents or caregivers of teenage BPD patients who seem out of control.

Because people with BPD are more likely to suffer frequent and recurring crises, family members are more likely to experience "compassion fatigue," Sympathy for their loved one gets dulled as a coping strategy.

4.1 Struggles Families of BPD Patients Experience

The burden of coping with a loved one's symptoms of BPD is made hard by managing their therapy. Clinicians often turn to the BPD family for assistance in organizing the family member's therapy, which may include numerous providers and teams and various levels of care (including occasional partial, outpatient treatment or inpatient hospitalization).

Family members may be asked to detect changes in their loved one's condition (for example, is their mood lower than normal or have they stopped taking their medicines as prescribed?), offer transportation to appointments, or coordinate the search for new treatment alternatives. Negotiating these issues and the broader mental health system is no simple job, and it may add to the stress of a family dealing with BPD.

4.2 Stress on the Family

Seeing a loved one suffer from BPD and coping with BPD's very challenging relationship symptoms may be extremely distressing for family members. When witnessing a loved one with BPD engage in self-destructive behaviors, family members frequently feel helpless. This is especially true for parents or caregivers of teenagers with BPD, who may seem erratic.

Many members of the BPD family may suffer significant psychological trauma as a result of some of the behaviors that are high-risk associated with BPD, in addition to the stressful situations of caring for a loved one with BPD.

Many individuals with BPD, for example, engage in self-harming activities such as cutting or burning. These habits may escalate to the point where they result in death by accident. Furthermore, individuals with BPD have an extremely high suicide rate.

Family members are often the ones who have to deal with these high-risk activities (e.g., transporting a loved one to the ER after a suicide attempt) and may suffer psychological distress as a result (which can lead to problems in several cases such as post-traumatic stress disorder).

4.3 Responsibility and Guilt

Many family members of individuals with BPD report their problems with guilt as being very challenging. According to research on the etiology of BPD, childhood maltreatment in the form of abuse or neglect may be linked to the development of BPD.

There is also evidence of a significant hereditary component. Family members and relatives, particularly parents, feel guilty or blame themselves due to these findings, even though the development of disorder in their loved one was beyond their control.

Along with internal conflicts over who is to blame for BPD development, many family members struggle to understand what role they have in their loved one's rehabilitation.

Some families attempt to be helpful, but they are worried that by doing so, they may be rewarding some of the BPD-related behaviors, such as self-harm. Others want to be helpful but are irritated by the person with BPD's behavior.

Finally, due to their own mental problems, some people find it difficult to be helpful. Because BPD tends to run in families, other members of the family may also be affected.

4.4 Getting Help

It is not always simple for family members to get the assistance and support they need to care for a loved one who has BPD. There are alternatives and services accessible if you are serious about seeking assistance. To begin, if you think your loved one has BPD and they have not yet sought therapy, you may urge them to do so.

BPD is a severe mental disease that requires expert assistance; you cannot help your loved one on your own.

There are additional materials available that are especially for family members. The Family Connections Program, for example, is offered throughout the United States by the National Alliance for Borderline Personality Disorder (NEA-BPD).

This 12-week course is intended to provide information, skill training, and support to family members of individuals who have BPD.

4.5 Broader Effects

Unfortunately, having a person with BPD in the family may cause stress, difficulties, and support problems for both immediate and extended family members. The tremendous stress caring for a kid with BPD may bring into a marital relationship is reported by parents of adolescents and adults with BPD.

This amount of stress is not unusual to cause tension in a marriage and separation or divorce.

Siblings are also impacted in a variety of ways. Some siblings may be drawn into a caring relationship, while others may withdraw from the family to protect themselves (or their own children, marriages, etc.) or to escape the emotional pain that comes with being in a close connection with someone with BPD.

Grandparents, uncles, aunts, and other relatives are all part of the BPD family support system, and they may feel the burden of caring for someone with BPD.

4.6 Making a relationship work when one of you has BPD

If you or your partner suffers from BPD, you can learn to deal with the emotional cycles that the disorder creates. This may aid in the development of a stronger, more resilient relationship.

WAYS TO IMPROVE BPD RELATIONSHIPS

- **Learn about BPD.** Understanding what a partner with BPD is going through is an important aspect of caring for them. Understanding the severity of their mental distress may help you react in a manner that keeps both of you safe from more chaos.

- **Offer emotional support.** Because of their history, someone with BPD may feel extremely lonely. Offer your spouse patience and understanding. It is feasible for them to improve their conduct and learn better behaviors.

- **Seek professional help.** People with BPD may benefit from therapy to help them better handle feelings and situations that distress them. Therapy may also help partners of individuals with BPD. A professional may assist a partner in understanding how to respond, comprehend, and support their spouse.

4.7 What if you are in a relationship with someone with BPD?

A romantic relationship with someone who has BPD may be turbulent. It is not uncommon to have a lot of turmoil and disorder in your life.

People with BPD, on the other hand, maybe very loving, empathetic, and affectionate. Some individuals enjoy this level of commitment from a relationship. A person suffering from BPD may also be extremely physically active and anxious to spend as much time as possible with their spouse.

People with BPD are sensitive to abandonment or rejection. Many people are hyperaware of indications that a love partner is unhappy or about to leave them.

When a person with BPD detects a change in their partner's emotions, genuine or imagined, they may retreat quickly. They may get enraged and upset over something that would not bother someone without BPD. They may even develop obsessive habits.

These emotional reversals may be tough to deal with. They may sometimes result in unsettling public situations. A person with BPD's impulsive conduct may put them or their spouse in danger.

The stability of a spouse, on the other hand, may have a beneficial impact on the emotional sensitivity that individuals with BPD have. Long-term relationships and marriages are feasible for individuals with BPD, but they may take a lot of effort from both **sides**.

4.8 Relationships over social media

Social media is an important part of modern life, and individuals with a borderline personality disorder may behave differently on it than others who do not.

Individuals with this disease, for example, interact more with others on social media and are more likely to regret expressing themselves on social media than people without this condition, according to a 2020 study. This regret may stem from the poster not getting the desired attention (positive or negative).

Because they acted impulsively, the individual may be more prone to regret their actions.

According to the research, people with borderline personality disorder are also more inclined to a friend and then unfriend or block other social media users. However, since individuals with this disease are more prone to befriend abusive people, this increased propensity to unfriend or block other users may be an effort to distance themselves from them.

Despite their interpersonal difficulties, individuals with borderline personality disorder can establish a social media connection network.

This may be because social media enables individuals to reconcile with others via the computer rather than face to face, which may seem less threatening, according to the research.

4.9 What if a patient with BPD has kids?

Although BPD may make parenting difficult, you can still be a good parent.

The greatest thing you can do for your children is to keep working on your therapy to get well and to protect them from the consequences of BPD as much as possible.

If you believe you need assistance with parenting, a parenting program may be able to assist you in learning new skills. Request assistance from your psychiatrist or another medical expert.

If you have a kid, you should keep him or her with you even if you have to go to the hospital.

4.10 Outlook for relationship

People with BPD may have healthy relationships because they are kind and caring. It requires effort, and there will always be difficulties.

Therapists and physicians may create a treatment plan with you or your partner. These medical professionals may assist you in addressing the BPD symptoms that are the most harmful to you and your relationship.

4.11 What does it take to feel better?

The severity of borderline personality disorder varies. Treatment success is determined by the severity of the disease and your level of understanding.

If you have insight and are diagnosed with a disease, you will research it and comprehend it. And what you learn will have an impact on you.

After then, therapy may help you find new methods to improve yourself and your relationships.

You may dislike — and resist — the diagnosis if you don't have much insight. A diagnosis of borderline personality disorder is a surprise for some and an insult for others.

4.12 borderline personality disorder during pregnancy

The risk of gestational diabetes, caesarian section, and premature rupture of the membranes, venous thromboembolism, chorioamnionitis, and preterm birth has been shown to be higher in women who have borderline personality disorder during their pregnancies. Women with BPD may feel discomfort when touched, see birth as traumatic and often desire an early delivery;

comorbidity with drug addiction is prevalent, and referral rates to child protective services are high. For women who are pregnant and suffer from a borderline personality disorder, it is recommended that they speak with their doctor or midwife about how they feel. Also, let them know if there is anything about the care you are getting that you are uncomfortable with. Patients with borderline personality disorder who are pregnant are often treated by a multidisciplinary team of health experts, which may include mental health services.

Chapter 5: How to improve social relations?

Do you have a family member or friend who has been diagnosed with BPD? While you cannot make someone get therapy, you can enhance communication, establish appropriate boundaries, and keep your relationship stable.

People with borderline personality disorder (BPD) often have difficult romantic and platonic relationships. For individuals with BPD and their partners, romantic relationships present a particular set of difficulties.

BPD symptoms may induce mood swings regularly.

For example, a person with BPD may love and doting one minute and then change their emotional state the next. They may feel suffocated or overburdened. This may cause them to push away the partner with whom they were just becoming closer.

People with BPD may have successful relationships with the help of therapy and ongoing support from family and partners. Continue reading to learn how it is possible to improve social relations if suffering from BPD.

5.1 What you need to know about BPD!

Relationships are challenging for people with borderline personality disorder (BPD), particularly those closest to them. Their erratic mood swings, rage outbursts, chronic abandonment anxieties, and impulsive and illogical actions may make loved ones feel powerless, mistreated, and out of sorts. Partners and family members often describe relationships with BPD individuals as an emotional roller coaster with no end in sight. You may feel helpless in the face of your loved one's BPD symptoms, imprisoned until you leave the relationship, or the individual seeks treatment. However, you have more power than you realize.

You may improve your relationship by controlling your own emotions, setting strong boundaries, and increasing communication with your loved one. Although there is no cure for BPD, with the proper therapy and support, many individuals with the disorder may improve, and their relationships can become more secure and fulfilling. Patients who have the greatest support and stability at home tend to recover faster than those who have more turbulent and insecure relationships.

You can enhance both the relationship and your personal quality of life if your spouse, parent, sibling, child, friend, or other loved one has BPD, even if the person with BPD cannot recognize the issue or seek therapy.

5.2 Learning all you can

It is critical to notice your loved one's suffering if he or she has a borderline personality disorder. The self-destructive and harmful actions are a result of profound emotional anguish. To put it another way, they aren't about you. Understand that when your loved one acts or says anything harmful to you, it is usually driven by a desire to alleviate the suffering they are feeling; it is seldom done on purpose.

Learning about BPD won't fix your relationship issues for you, but it will help you understand what you are up against and deal with challenges more constructively.

5.3 Recognizing the symptoms and signs of BPD

It is not always simple to identify the signs and symptoms of borderline personality disorder. Small things may frequently provoke strong emotions in your family member or loved one who suffers from BPD.

Borderline individuals are often unable to think clearly or healthily calm themselves once upset. They may say things that are unpleasant or behave in unsafe or improper ways. Family members, lovers, and friends may experience stress as a result of their emotional instability.

Many individuals who have a close connection with someone who has BPD are aware that something is wrong with their loved one but don't know what it is or whether it even has a name.

Is someone you care about suffering from borderline personality disorder?

In your relationship:

1. Do you feel compelled to walk on eggshells around your loved one, monitoring everything you say and do in case you irritate them? Do you frequently keep your thoughts and emotions hidden in order to prevent conflicts and damaged feelings?

2. Does your loved one go from one emotional extreme to the other very instantly? Are they calm one minute, enraged the next, and then depressed all of a sudden? Is it possible that these erratic mood swings are unexpected and irrational?

3. Does your significant other see you as either all good or all terrible, with no in-between? For instance, you might be "perfect" and the one person they can rely on, or you could be "selfish" and "unfeeling" and have never really loved them.

4. Do you ever feel as if you cannot win, as if everything you say or do will be twisted and used against you? Do you ever feel that your loved one's expectations are shifting all the time, and you are not sure how to maintain the peace?

5. Do you have to take responsibility for everything? Do you find yourself being scolded and punished

for things that make no sense? Is the individual accusing you of something you didn't do or say? When you attempt to explain or reassure your spouse, do you feel misunderstood?

6. Do you ever feel like you are being controlled by fear, guilt, or outlandish behavior? When they believe you are unhappy or about to leave, does your loved one fly into violent rages, make threats, make theatrical declarations, or do dangerous things?

If you answered yes to the majority of these questions, your partner or family member may be suffering from borderline personality disorder.

5.4 Things People with Borderline Personality Disorder Want You to Know

People suffering from borderline personality disorder are often misunderstood. You can help them by trying to understand them.

Emotionally unstable personality disorder, often known as borderline personality disorder, is a personality disorder that affects how you think and feels about yourself and others.

Borderline personality disorder (BPD) is characterized by a high fear of abandonment, difficulty maintaining good relationships, intense emotions, impulsive behavior, and even paranoia and detachment.

It may be a frightening disease to live with, which is why individuals with BPD need to be surrounded by people who understand and support them. It is, nevertheless, a highly stigmatized disease.

Many individuals with the disorder are afraid to come out about it since there are many misunderstandings about it.

But it is something we want to change.

Here are some of the things that people with BPD want others to understand:

1. 'Even when things are going well, we are afraid you'll leave. We despise it as well.'

Fear of abandonment is one of the most common symptoms of BPD, and it may arise even when things in the relationship appear to be going well.

Even though it seems illogical to others, the worry that others will abandon them or that they aren't good enough for that person may feel very genuine to the suffering.

Someone with BPD will go to any length to prevent this from occurring, which is why they may seem "clingy" or "needy." Though it may be difficult to understand, keep in mind that it comes from a place of fear, which may be very tough to live with.

2. 'Everything is hot and terrible to touch as if you are walking through life with third-degree emotional burns.'

People with BPD have very strong emotions that may last anywhere from a few hours to several days, and they shift rapidly.

For example, we may go from being very joyful to feeling extremely depressed and sad. BPD may seem like walking on eggshells around oneself at times; we never know how our mood will swing, and it can be difficult to manage.

Even if we seem to be "overly sensitive," keep in mind that we don't always have control.

3. 'Everything is more strongly felt, whether it be good, bad, or otherwise. Our response to such emotions may seem out of proportion, yet it is in our thoughts appropriate.'

BPD may be very intense as if vacillating between two extremes. Both we and others around us may get exhausted as a result of this.

But it is essential to realize that whatever the person with BPD is thinking at the moment is perfectly acceptable in their view. So don't tell them that they are being foolish or make them feel like their emotions aren't real.

It may take you some time to process their ideas, but things may seem terrifying at the moment. This entails not passing judgment and, where necessary, providing space and time.

4. 'I don't have multiple personalities.'

BPD is often mistaken with dissociative identity disorder, in which individuals acquire many personalities since it is a personality disorder.

This, however, is not the case. BPD patients do not have many personalities. BPD is a personality disorder in which you struggle with how you feel and think about yourself and other people, and as a consequence, you are experiencing issues in your life.

That isn't to say that dissociative identity disorder should be stigmatized, but it should be distinguished from other disorders.

5. 'We aren't in any way harmful or manipulative... All we need is a little more love.'

BPD still has a lot of stigmas attached to it. Because of their symptoms, many people still think that individuals who suffer from it are manipulative or dangerous.

While this may be true for a small percentage of individuals with BPD, the majority of people with BPD are just suffering from their sense of self and relationships.

It is essential to remember that none of them are harmful. In reality, individuals who have mental illness are more prone than others to hurt themselves.

6. 'It is draining and irritating. It is also very difficult to locate high-quality, low-cost therapy.'

Many individuals with BPD go untreated, but it is not because they don't want to be helped. It is because this mental disease isn't addressed the same way other mental illnesses are.

For one thing, BPD isn't treated with medications. Only therapy, such as dialectical behavioral therapy (DBT) and cognitive-behavioral therapy (CBT), may help (CBT). There are no medicines that have been shown to be helpful in the treatment of BPD (though in some cases, medications are used off-label in order to relieve symptoms).

It is also true that some doctors think individuals with BPD would be difficult patients because of the stigma, making finding successful therapy difficult.

Intensive DBT programs may help many individuals with BPD, but they aren't always easy to find. That is to say, don't be quick to criticize someone with BPD if they aren't "getting better" - seeking treatment is difficult enough.

7. 'We aren't unlovable, and we do know how to love.'

BPD patients have a lot of love to offer, to the point where it may be overpowering.

Relationships may be a whirlwind when someone with BPD — particularly those who struggle with persistent feelings of emptiness or loneliness — finds a genuine connection; the thrill can be as strong as any other emotion.

This may make it tough to be in a relationship with someone who has BPD, but it also indicates that this person has a lot of love to give. They just want to know that their emotions are reciprocated, and they may need further assurance to guarantee that the connection remains satisfying for both of you.

If you are in a relationship or have a loved one with BPD, it is essential to educate yourself on the disorder and be cautious of stereotypes.

Suppose you read anything regarding BPD that you would

not like to be stated about you. In that case, chances are a person with borderline personality disorder won't benefit from the same assumption being made about them.

It may make or break a relationship if you work to acquire a sympathetic knowledge of what they are going through and how you might assist them and you manage.

If you need additional help, tell someone how you fee — its better if it is a clinician or therapist! — so they can provide you with support and advice on how to improve your mental health.

Remember that providing the greatest possible support for your loved one begins with taking the best possible care of yourself.

5.5 If You Want to Help Someone with BPD, First, You Have to Take Care of Yourself

It is all too easy to get caught up in heroic attempts to satisfy and appease a family member or spouse who has a borderline personality disorder. You may find yourself devoting most of your attention to the person with BPD, neglecting your own emotional needs in the process. This, on the other hand, is a formula for bitterness, despair, exhaustion, and even illness.

When you are exhausted and overwhelmed by stress, you cannot assist others or maintain long-term, fulfilling relationships. You must "put on your own oxygen mask first," just as you would in an in-flight emergency.

You are allowed (and in fact encouraged) to have a life! Allow yourself to have a life apart from your connection with the individual who has BPD. It is not self-indulgent to set aside time to unwind and enjoy yourself. Your new viewpoint will benefit both of you when you return to your BPD relationship.

Don't neglect your own physical health. When you are in the middle of a relationship crisis, it is easy to overlook eating well, exercising, and getting enough sleep. Try to stay away from this trap. You'll be better equipped to manage stress and regulate your emotions and actions if you are healthy and well-rested.

Avoid the temptation to isolate. Make it a priority to keep in contact with loved ones who make you happy. You need the assistance of individuals who make you feel cared for, will listen to you, and provide you with reality checks when necessary.

You can join a support group for family members of patients of BPD. Meeting with people who understand your situation may be very beneficial. If you cannot locate an in-person support group in your region, you may wish to join an online BPD support group.

Learn to manage anxiety. In reaction to bad behavior, being worried or angry can only exacerbate your loved one's rage or agitation. You may learn to alleviate tension as it occurs and remain cool and relaxed as the strain rises by practicing with sensory input.

5.6 Remember the 3 C's rule

Many friends or family members feel terrible and blame themselves for the borderline person's harmful conduct. You may wonder what you did to enrage the individual, believe you deserve the abuse or blame yourself for any treatment failure or relapse.

However, keep in mind that you are not accountable for anybody else. BPD patients are in charge of their own actions and behaviors.

The 3 Cs are:

1. I cannot **cure** it.

2. I didn't **cause** it.

3. I cannot **control** it.

5.7 How to communicate with someone who has BPD

Any relationship requires communication but talking with a borderline person may be particularly difficult. People in close relationships with borderline adults often compare conversing with them to fight with a young kid. People with BPD have difficulty interpreting body language and comprehending a conversation's nonverbal substance. They may make harsh, unjust, or illogical statements. Their fear of desertion may lead them to overreact to every perceived insult, no matter how little, and their anger might manifest itself in rash outbursts, verbal abuse, or even violence.

For individuals with BPD, the issue is that the illness distorts both the signals they receive and their attempt to convey. Randi Kreger, a BPD specialist and author, compares it to "getting 'aural dyslexia,'. In aural dyslexia they hear words and phrases backward, sideways, inside out, and without context."

One of the most effective methods to assist someone with BPD in relaxing is to listen to them and acknowledge their emotions. You may help defuse attacks and rages and create a deeper, closer connection by understanding how a borderline person hears you and adjusting how you interact with them.

5.8 Communication tips

It is critical to know when it is appropriate to initiate a discussion. It is not the moment to speak with your loved one if they are enraged, verbally abusive, or making violent threats. It is preferable to gently postpone the discussion by stating, "Let's speak later when we are both calm." or" I want to offer you my full attention, but it is very difficult for me right now."

When things are calmer:

Talk about other things. Make time to investigate and share other hobbies so that you and your loved one may live lives that aren't exclusively defined by the disorder. Discussions about lighter topics may assist in defusing tensions between you and inspire your partner to pursue new interests or reignite old ones.

Focus on the emotions and not the words. The emotions of someone with BPD convey much more than the words he or she uses. People suffering from BPD need affirmation and acknowledgment of their suffering. Listen to the feeling your loved one is seeking to express without getting caught up in trying to reconcile the words spoken.

Distractions such as the television, computer, or mobile phone should be avoided. Avoid interrupting or diverting the discussion to your own problems. Set aside your judgment, refrain from assigning blame or criticism, and show interest in what is being stated by nodding or making short verbal remarks such as "yeah" or "oh huh." You don't have to agree with what the other person says to show that you are paying attention and sympathizing.

Try to make the person feel heard and understood. Even if what they are saying is completely illogical, don't point out how you think they are incorrect, attempt to win the debate, or dismiss their emotions.

Try to stay calm, even when the person is acting out. Avoid becoming defensive in the face of accusations and critiques, no matter how unjust they may seem to be. Defending yourself will simply enrage your partner. If you need to get some time and space to relax, take a step back.

Try to distract them when emotions rise. Anything that attracts your loved one's attention may help, but the most effective distraction is when the activity is also calming. Exercising, drinking hot tea, grooming a pet, listening to music, gardening, painting, or doing home tasks are good options.

5.9 How to set and reinforce healthy boundaries?

Talk about limits with your partner when you are both calm and not in the middle of an argument. Make it plain what conduct you will and will not accept from the individual. "If you cannot speak to me without shouting insults at me, I'll walk out," you may say to a loved one.

Do...

- When establishing boundaries, reassure the individual with BPD calmly. "I love you and want our relationship to succeed, but I cannot take the stress created by your actions," you might say. I'm counting on you to make this adjustment for me."

- Ensure everyone in the family understands the rules—and how to enforce them if they are broken.

- Setting limits should be seen as a process rather than a single occurrence. Rather than bombarding your partner with a large list of restrictions all at once, present them one or two at a time.

Don't...

Make ultimatums and threats that you know you won't be able to keep. Your loved one will test the boundaries you set inevitably, as is human nature. If you give in and don't enforce the penalties, your loved one will understand that the barrier is worthless and will continue to act badly. Ultimatums are only used as a final option (you should also be prepared to follow through).

Allow abusive conduct to continue. No one should be subjected to verbal or physical assault. The fact that a personality disorder causes your loved one's conduct does not make it any less genuine or harmful to you or other family members.

Protect the person with BPD from the consequences of their behavior to enable them. You may need to leave if your loved one refuses to respect your limits and continues to make you feel uncomfortable. It doesn't mean you don't care about them, but you should always prioritize your own well-being.

5.10 Setting healthy boundaries with a borderline loved one

Setting and enforcing appropriate limits or boundaries is one of the most effective methods to assist a loved one with borderline personality disorder gain control over their behavior. Setting boundaries may help your loved one cope with the expectations of the world, where schools, the legal system, workplaces all establish and enforce strict limits on what is and isn't acceptable conduct.

Setting boundaries in your relationship may offer you more options for how to respond when faced with bad conduct, replacing the instability and chaos of your current scenario with a feeling of order. You'll be able to establish a feeling of respect and trust between you if both sides respect the limits, which are essential components in every meaningful relationship.

Setting limits, on the other hand, isn't a quick cure for a broken relationship. Things may become worse before they get better at first. BPD patients are afraid of rejection and are sensitive to every perceived insult. If you have never established limits in your relationship before, your partner is likely to respond negatively when you do. If you give in to your loved one's anger or abuse, you'll simply be encouraging their bad behavior and perpetuating the pattern. Maintaining your resolve and sticking to your choices, on the other hand, may strengthen you, help your loved one, and eventually change your relationship.

5.11 Supporting your loved one's BPD treatment

Although borderline personality disorder is extremely curable, many individuals with the condition refuse to seek help or deny that they have a problem. Even if this is the case with a loved one, you may still provide support, enhance communication, and establish boundaries while encouraging your family member or friend to get professional assistance.

While medication choices are limited, a skilled therapist's assistance may make a significant impact on your loved one's rehabilitation. Schema-focused therapy and Dialectical Behavior Therapy (DBT) are two BPD treatments that may help your loved one work through relationship and trust problems and learn new coping strategies. They may learn to quiet down the emotional and psychological turmoil and self-soothe in positive ways in therapy.

5.12 How to support treatment?

If your loved one refuses to admit that they have BPD, you may want to seek couple's counseling. Rather than focusing on your loved one's disorder, the emphasis here is on connecting and encouraging improved communication. Your spouse may be more willing to consent to this and, in the future, seek BPD treatment.

Help your loved one to try mindfulness and relaxation methods like deep breathing, yoga, or meditation to learn how to deal with stress and emotions healthily. They may also use sensory-based stimulation to alleviate stress in the present. You may engage in any of these treatments alongside your loved ones, which can improve your connection and motivate them to seek further therapy options.

Your loved one may learn to press pause when the desire to act out or act impulsively hits by developing the capacity to endure discomfort.

5.13 Setting goals for BPD recovery - Go slowly

It is important to be patient and establish reasonable objectives while helping a loved one heal. Change can and can occur, but it takes time, as it does with reversing any kind of behavior habit.

- Instead of striving for big, unachievable objectives that would set you and your loved one up for disappointment and frustration, take small steps. You both will have a better chance of success if you reduce your expectations and establish small, achievable objectives.

- Supporting the rehabilitation of a loved one may be both difficult and rewarding. You must look for yourself, but the process may help you develop as a person and improve your relationship.

Chapter 6: Workplace and BPD

If you have been diagnosed with BPD, you are probably scared and concerned about how it will affect your life, particularly your job. Despite the fact that BPD symptoms may make things more difficult, many individuals with this disorder go on to have very excellent careers.

6.1 Working with BPD

Someone with a borderline personality disorder may intuitively hide any traces of an emotional struggle. When you add in a natural desire to please others (along with a heaping spoonful of perfectionism), it is easy to isolate and battle alone. This may lead to fatigue, overworking, and misunderstanding in the workplace. Strong communication and openness with management and coworkers are not always easy, but it can be a lifeline, a necessary tool to use as frequently as possible. You'll feel relieved after these meetings or phone conversations if you have the proper management. Remind yourself that you are just human, that you can only do so much, and that asking for assistance requires a certain degree of professional maturity.

Many individuals with BPD must battle an all-or-nothing mentality. They are especially prone to becoming absorbed by their job and tilting the balances of their work-life balance too far in a direction. They aren't always good at shrugging their shoulders, embracing what they cannot change, or seeing the larger picture. Taking frequent work breaks, whether at home or in a crowded workplace, may help you manage this. Never underestimate the value of a lunchtime walk or a short conversation by the office kettle. BPD may cause us to be hyperaware of our environment. Taking a break from your inbox may assist in relieving any tension, anxiety, or emotion that is building up.

The disorder may harm the capacity to separate emotion from our job. You may never say things like, "It is simply business." Everything is personal to you. We've all been frustrated by getting a nasty email or a blunt answer. This may be catastrophic for someone with BPD. They are very sensitive to everything. Therefore, a dismissive email may make or ruin your day. It sometimes takes an outside voice to bring you back to reality, so communicate – it is almost always the solution.

6.2 Effects of Symptoms and Signs of BPD at Work

When your symptoms do not overburden you, you can have a successful job. However, the consequences of BPD may change depending on the environment, impacting your job performance and capacity to "fit in" with your colleagues.

BPD symptoms may have a variety of consequences for your job. Your self-image, objectives, and even preferences may often vary if you have BPD, making it difficult to commit to a single professional path. Because you may lose out on promotions or chances related to seniority because of your shaky self-image or sense of self, you may fall behind in terms of career advancement.

Many individuals with BPD have the tendency to view people and circumstances as either all-good or all-bad, which is known as an all-or-nothing mentality or splitting. For example, you might begin with what you consider to be your ideal work. Then you get a bad performance evaluation or make a mistake one day.

Instead of viewing this as something you can fix and overcome, you may get totally discouraged and give up on your ideal career. Workplace relationships may be harmed by often shifting emotions and all-or-nothing thinking, resulting in unstable partnerships and divisive workplaces.

BPD symptoms may also make it difficult to concentrate, which can contribute to poor job performance. Dissociation, for example, may make it difficult to complete activities in a timely manner.

6.3 Finding the Best Job for You

For individuals with BPD, there is no such thing as a "best" job. It is very dependent on the circumstances of the person. Everyone's symptoms are unique, and a job that suits you may not suit someone else, and vice versa.

The most essential thing is to choose a career that you like. Here are some things to think about while choosing which kind of work is best for you:

Schedule: Part-time employment or a job with a flexible schedule are excellent alternatives if you believe you'll need time off for doctor's visits or therapy sessions. Furthermore, daytime hours are ideal for maintaining a consistent sleep pattern.

Creativity: When given a chance to be creative, many individuals with BPD flourish. Having a job that requires you to be creative may prevent you from being bored.

Workplace: What kind of setting do you thrive in? Some individuals thrive in a calm, peaceful environment where they can easily focus, while others thrive when there are many activities going on at once. The trick is to locate an atmosphere that will encourage you to succeed. Workplaces that are stressful and unsupportive may aggravate mental health issues.

6.4 Get to Know Yourself

The most essential aspect of choosing a fulfilling career is self-awareness. You should be aware of the following facts about yourself:

- Values

- Limitations and triggers

- Interests

- Personality traits

- Skills

- Physical abilities

- Strengths

6.5 How to Cope with BPD in the Workplace

Some strategies for dealing with the pressures of daily life include:

- Avoid being in a stressful scenario. Taking a step back from a potentially unpleasant scenario may help you view things more clearly. It also allows you to improve your positive communication skills, which is particularly essential in professional interactions.

- Take your medicine as prescribed and follow all of your appointments. Even if you believe you are feeling better, it is critical that you take the medications given to you and maintain your doctor's visits. Before discontinuing or changing your medication, always check with your doctor. Work with your therapist to find a good balance between your work and your regular appointments.

- Try some relaxing exercises. If you ever find yourself in a frustrating situation, relaxation methods such as meditation and deep breathing may help you retain some stability.

6.6 Building a Strong Career

These are all factors to consider while deciding on a professional path. It is possible that you are having issues in all of these areas or just one or two. Consider how these symptoms may affect your capacity to operate in your chosen profession daily. If you have many stress issues, for example, selecting a job in a fast-paced, high-stress sector may be a bad idea.

It is possible that a quieter, calmer, or more relaxing atmosphere might be beneficial for you. At the same time, you shouldn't let your diagnosis dictate or restrict your career options entirely. There are individuals with BPD who have excelled in every field imaginable. When assessing your strengths and shortcomings, keep in mind your symptoms and realize that you are a person distinct from your condition.

Speak with your therapist if you are concerned about how your symptoms may affect your job. They may be able to provide you with some helpful symptom management techniques as well as recommendations for possible job choices that fit your skills.

6.7 Some Tips for Working Excellently with BPD

Have you ever had a strange discussion with someone that made you doubt your own ability to see things? This is often the case while dealing with individuals who have borderline personality disorder as a professional helper (BPD). It may be a very unsettling experience for anybody, especially if you pride yourself on your strong intuition and interpersonal abilities.

Therapists have an encounter with patients who responded with, "Are you kidding me?". or "Why would I consider such a thing?!" Despite the fact that the therapists are aware of their BPD symptoms.

Pervasive perceptual changes and abnormal responses to such perceptions are hallmarks of BPD. Because they continually see events and dealings differently from others around them, the individual tends to feel disconnected from others.

BPD affects how people perceive information, particularly when it comes to the intentions of others. As a result, these people often feel abandoned, rejected, misunderstood, criticized, inferior, and lonely. Conversations, unsurprisingly, are frequently unproductive, resulting in conflict and suffering for both parties.

The following pointers may assist you in more successfully navigating these frequently difficult conversations:

Build Trust

Although trust is necessary in every healthy relationship, being able to build trust with someone who has BPD is extremely necessary if you want to have a meaningful conversation. Because people with BPD have extremely sensitive personalities and see their early connections as invalidating, their capacity to trust others may be severely harmed. Before you start challenging, as a helper, make sure to concentrate on establishing connection and trust. It doesn't matter if you are right if you cannot connect.

One approach to build trust is to repeatedly emphasize that you are there to assist the person and will do all possible to make them feel secure. Assuring remarks like "I care about you and your best interests" and "It is essential to me that you feel understood" may help. It is also important to remember that trust is earned via our deeds rather than our words. You can strive to accomplish this by being dependable, empathetic, and straightforward.

Validate

To help someone with BPD, we must strike a balance between empathy and establishing boundaries. You may learn to utilize empathy to improve your tolerance if you are aware that the person tends to live in continuous emotional anguish that distorts their view of reality. This will enable you to see if the person genuinely believes their charges or insults at the time. Validating enables us to show that we comprehend their point of view without necessarily agreeing with it.

You should let them know that you are trying to understand how they view the world when you say, "I understand why you feel that way" or "You have a right to your own emotions and ideas." This not only helps to establish trust, but it also improves the chances of expressing oneself in relation to your own needs and perceptions.

Assert Yourself

Accepting improper behavior is not the same as providing support and affirmation to someone with BPD. Regardless of how the person reacts, it is critical that you retain your own sense of reality. You may need to reaffirm that your ideas, emotions, and limits are your own. After you have reminded someone that you care about them and acknowledged their viewpoint, it is essential to let them know that you have a different perspective on the issue. For instance, "Feeling invisible is a horrible feeling," Due to other obligations, I informed you two weeks ago that we would not be able to meet this week. It is important to me that I'm accessible to my clients and that I give them plenty of notice if I have to cancel."

To help someone with BPD, we must strike a balance between empathy and establishing boundaries.

When dealing with someone who has perceptual problems, part of expressing oneself is stating our requirements in specific terms and letting them know what will happen if our boundaries are challenged. Instead of stating, "I don't like when you waste my time," we may add, "It is essential to me that we finish our session at 12:00 because if we meet any later, I won't have enough time with my next client." I owe that customer more time for their next appointment, which must come from your time." Although the person may disagree with your limits, the expectation and result have been communicated to prevent misunderstandings.

The following is an example of how trust-building, validation, and assertion may be used to communicate: "I'm concerned about you. I realize how frustrating it is when I am unavailable when you call for help, but as a therapist, I need to make sure that I am accessible for other clients. As a result, I must maintain our current communication schedule. Your comments and criticism are upsetting to me, and I'd want to speak with you about alternative methods to express your dissatisfaction."

Strong relationships require reliable connections, the capacity to be heard and understood, and open and honest communication about needs and limitations. These concepts are crucial when interacting with someone who has BPD symptoms. If you are in a relationship with someone who has perceptual issues, do your best to support them while also looking after your health and well-being. If we are tired and angry, we cannot give others what they need.

6.8 Helping an employee with BPD

An employer must provide as much stability as possible to an employee with BPD in order to maintain a stable work environment. Rather than singling out particular behaviors and focusing on expectations from all workers, try to appreciate each employee's peculiarities and personalities as possible assets in the organization. Although impulsive or disruptive behavior may occasionally be overt, the problems typically emerge in more subtle ways.

Demonstrate emotional validation while being polite... Do not overstep your bounds and make an effort to record everything.

Interacting with people who have BPD may be difficult. Therefore, it is important to establish clear boundaries and emphasize appropriate professional behavior and remind coworkers to complete given duties and consider their emotions. It may be essential to explain the proper time and location for various interactions such as meetings, issues, and complaints. Prepare for objections as well as the chance that the employee may get enraged for unexplained reasons. Remember to keep meetings from devolving into infighting. Demonstrate emotional validation while being polite. You don't necessarily want to support an employee's point of view; rather, you want to validate the emotions associated with that point of view - "I hear you" or "I understand how you feel." Do not overstep your bounds and make an effort to record everything.

If your attempts to manage a BPD employee or colleague are unsuccessful, call your company's Employee Assistance Program coordinator for assistance. You may tell the individual with BPD that is talking to someone via the Employee Assistance Program could help them get through a difficult time or cope with a problem.

People with BPD have challenging emotional experiences on a daily basis, and they may need professional therapy to acquire adaptive methods for managing symptoms that interfere with their ability to function productively. Encourage the person to get appropriate therapy if they do so since you may be investing in a high-potential employee and creating an open and healthy work atmosphere.

6.9 Some Tips for Working with Clients with Borderline Personality Disorder

Clients with (BPD) suffer from continuous "emotion dysregulation" (broad mood swings, unexpected rage, needless suspiciousness, excessively strong excitement, misdirected love emotions, and so on). Unless they are learning to manage their emotions in treatment, this is not something they have conscious control over. In fact, emotion dysregulation is at the root of most of their difficulties in relationships, including with romantic partners, family members, and coworkers. In light of this, here are seven suggestions for individuals who work with people who have BPD:

1. **Create a sense of us.** Rather than getting into a fight or expressing your frustrations with the client, strive to establish a sense of us: "forming a team against the issue," rather than "me versus you." Keep your attention on the following step and how it will benefit you. Avoid expressing anger at these clients since it may cause them to experience strong, unmanageable emotions. They are typically better at handling rage than you are. If you do get angry with them, try to cool down immediately and explain that you didn't mean to criticize or blame them and that you'd want to move on to the next job. Avoid using energy in self-defense. They hold the majority of their issues inside themselves, causing many of your conflicts—but they cannot recognize or accept it. Just remember: It is not about you and go on to the next job.

2. **Focus on the future.** In general, people with BPD generate disputes, crises, confusion, and anxiety in their lives without recognizing it or comprehending their role in creating these events. Focusing on their previous

behavior—or allowing them to get trapped in the past—will only serve to reinforce and exacerbate these issues. Instead, recognize that the person's history was tough, but concentrate on what they can accomplish today.

3. Stay calm. You don't have to go on an emotional roller coaster just because your client is. Your client will frequently calm down if you keep a pleasant, calm, and comforting tone of voice and body language. They will reflect your feelings. In other words, being furious with your client for being angry, unreasonable, stubborn, self-contradictory, and so on will just exacerbate their out-of-control emotions.

4. Be empathetic. EAR Statements are a technique of soothing and engaging with angry customers that we teach in our High Conflict Institute training. The EAR is an acronym meaning Empathy, Attention, and Respect. Anyone sad will find a statement that contains EAR to be comforting and useful. BPD sufferers value empathy above all else since they often feel judged, rejected, alone, and as if no one cares about how they feel. As a result, stress words demonstrate empathy and compassion, such as I understand your frustration. That must not be easy. On this, I'll collaborate with you. This is a perplexing circumstance. I understand that these are significant choices in your life. I want to assist you.

5.   Don't try to change them. You may believe you have figured out how to solve a lot of their problems: just quit doing this or that! However, this is likely to backfire. For one, they have a barrier to having insight into themselves (it is part of the disorder), so your "constructive comments" won't have them thinking about and reflecting on their previous conduct. Instead, it will keep them occupied with self-defense. Second, it will harm your working connection with them because it will seem to them that you dislike them that you believe there is something wrong with them to the point that you are condemning their previous conduct rather than embracing them for who they are. They've been exposed to this kind of constructive criticism for so long that you'll be surprised at how furious it makes them feel. After much criticism, your relationship may never completely recover.

6. Don't focus on feelings. Because their emotions are so difficult to control, it is essential to assist them in focusing on what they are thinking and on tasks. Asking them how they are feeling is a bad idea since they are typically feeling out-of-control, powerless, weak, vulnerable, and like a victim. You are more likely to develop out-of-control emotions if you put them in touch with their feelings. When making choices, rather than asking how they feel about something, ask what they think about it. Do not inquire as to why they acted in an unfavorable manner yesterday or last month. They often have no idea why, and it will almost certainly bring up their profound feeling of guilt or resentment over what they did.

7.   Focus on their choices now. Rather than starting a conversation on how terrible everything is or what they should have done better in the past, concentrate on what their options or alternatives are today. They don't have to defend themselves about the past if they concentrate on the options ahead of them. You may provide your opinion on which option is the best one, but you must acknowledge that they have a choice. Because individuals with BPD dislike being told what to do (they've had enough of it), giving them an option is powerful and supportive of their decision-making process. Do you want me to assist you, or do you want to attempt it on your own? Please respond by Thursday at 5 p.m. with a yes or no. You may not be able to control another person's conduct, but you may be able to influence the good or bad repercussions of their behavior. It may be beneficial to inform them of the possible implications of each decision but do it pleasantly so that it does not come across as a threat.

In summary, if you follow these basic guidelines, you can manage a professional relationship with someone who has BPD. Simply manage your connection and concentrate on what you need to do to aid them in solving their own issues with your support.

6.10 Accommodations for employees with BPD

Increasing your workplace's mental health confidence requires creating a friendly, positive, and inclusive atmosphere for everyone. Employers may provide a variety of adjustments for people with BPD. Some of these perks are meant to help you take care of yourself, decrease work-related stress, or promote good relationships with your colleagues and managers:

- Develop clear, documented work procedures and apply them to all employees fairly and equitably.

- Encourage people to go to counseling or psychotherapy sessions and provide flexible work schedules to accommodate them.

- Allow for phone calls or phone breaks to therapists and others for required assistance during work hours.

- Consider implementing a program that enables workers to work from home on certain days of the week.

- Allow workers to listen to calm, soothing music in their offices.

- Make space enclosures or a separate office available.

- For good work relationships, provide appropriate praise and encouragement.

- Make time for undisturbed work periods.

- Make an Employee Assistance Program available and encourage employees to utilize it.

- Provide written checklists and instructions

- Make daily "TO-DO" lists and cross things off as you do them.

- Reorganize big work responsibilities into smaller ones.

- Mark meetings and deadlines on several calendars.

- Mark meetings and deadlines on several calendars.

- Make a list of long-term and short-term objectives.

- Coworkers and managers should get sensitivity training.

- Encourage all workers to keep non-work-related discussions out of the workplace.

- Provide the employee with private weekly/monthly meetings to address workplace problems and performance.

- When an employee discusses workplace difficulties, use active listening skills. Always remember to validate your employees' feelings.

Chapter 7: Understanding Stigma When You Have BPD

A stigma is a preconceived notion or stereotype that leads someone to think less of or despise the person in question. People tend to remove themselves from stigmatized people, blame stigmatized individuals for bad behaviors, and discriminate against stigmatized individuals.

7.1 The Stigma of Mental Illness

Unfortunately, stigma is a problem that many people with mental disorders face, making it more difficult to get appropriate treatment. If you have a mental illness like borderline personality disorder, you must cope with both the symptoms of your condition and the assumptions of others.

Many people think of individuals with mental illnesses as dangerous, unstable, weak-willed, and untrustworthy because of how they are portrayed on television and in movies.

According to studies conducted by World Psychiatry, people's attitudes have been negatively influenced due to these portrayals of these diseases.

It has influenced how they see people with mental illnesses in three ways:

- They are afraid of mentally ill individuals because they think they threaten others and are prone to violent outbursts.

- Individuals also think that people with mental illness are self-indulgent and lazy and that if they simply quit wallowing, they would be cured of their illness.

- Others think that people who suffer from mental illnesses are childish and need the same level of care as a baby, incapable of making their own decisions. Furthermore, owing to social biases, many individuals with borderline personalities experience significant levels of self-stigma.

7.2 The Stigma Associated with Borderline Personality Disorder

Individuals with borderline personality disorder (BPD), like you, are among the most stigmatized of the major mental disorders. BPD is often misunderstood, even by healthcare experts.

BPD sufferers are often stereotyped as manipulative, dramatic, and attention-seeking. These preconceptions may lead therapists to ignore your symptoms or concerns, putting your health at risk. It may also obstruct therapy by making mental health professionals emotionally distant from their patients or reluctant to assist and participate therapeutically.

BPD is stigmatized, which may lead to misdiagnosis. Due to a lack of knowledge, people with borderline personality disorder are often diagnosed with bipolar disorder or severe depressive illness. Because the therapies for these diseases are so different, an incorrect diagnosis may be harmful to your health.

Because of these concerns, it is essential to locate a doctor or clinician who is well-versed in borderline personality disorder and current treatment guidelines.

7.3 Stigma's Impact on Treatment

This misconception may make finding steady employment, safe housing, and living a regular life more difficult for individuals receiving treatment. They are constantly accused of misbehavior, carelessness, or rage, and therefore find it difficult to establish a consistent routine.

Many individuals with mental problems try to conceal their condition because of the stigma attached to it, unwilling to acknowledge others or even themselves that anything is wrong.

Others may disregard their treatment, missing therapy sessions and medicine in order to keep their illness hidden. This may create severe setbacks in their treatment by creating considerable problems and delays.

Mental health stigma is extremely prevalent in society, and it is a continuous battle; many illnesses continue to be misunderstood. While some success has been achieved in the fight against prejudice, there is still much more work to be done. It is important to find a doctor who knows your requirements and form a support network of individuals you can trust while exploring treatment choices.

7.4 Manifestations of Borderline Personality Disorder Stigma

We have seen great attempts in the United States to de-stigmatize mental illness over the last few decades. These initiatives have frequently been very successful for illnesses such as anxiety, bipolar disorder, depression, and PTSD, bringing mental disorders out of the shadows and creating an atmosphere in which seeking borderline personality disorder therapy is regarded as a sign of courage and fortitude. Even in this environment, however, misconceptions and discriminatory attitudes against individuals with borderline personality disorder have generally persisted.

The stigma attached to borderline personality disorder stems in part from the disease's symptoms. The disorder's extreme emotional instability, as well as its effect on relationships, has left a lengthy trail of individuals who have seen and been harmed by it. Unlike depression, which is generally known to be a painful internal process, borderline personality disorder seems to radiate outward, producing significant social harm that may overwhelm and conceal the underlying suffering. Narratives about BPD often focus on the illness's "toxic" character and its consequences on bystanders rather than on individuals suffering from it. As a consequence, the existence of borderline personality is often viewed as a warning sign to others, rather as an excessively painful condition for the diagnosed individual: do not attempt to establish a connection with such a person, as it will only end in misery.

At the same time, borderline personality disorder has long been viewed as an unchangeable and untreatable aspect of one's personality, perpetuating stigma in both mainstream culture and the medical community; studies have shown that mental health professionals are "more prejudicial and judgmental toward patients with BPD [than] to other patients of mental health." People with BPD are often stereotyped as non-compliant with treatment, attention-seeking, antagonistic, demanding, manipulative, and, ultimately, treatment-resistant. Furthermore, some mental health providers refuse to treat individuals who have BPD. The mental health professionals who address borderline personality disorder frequently do so without the appropriate training, making sessions unpleasant and uncomfortable for everyone. Patients may feel criticized and misunderstood, while providers may feel useless and insufficient.

7.5 The Damage of Stigma

For individuals who have a borderline personality disorder, the stigma surrounding the illness has severe and devastating repercussions. Rejection, catholicization, and demonization may worsen relationship instability and social isolation when combined with BPD symptoms. At the same time, when prejudiced attitudes are internalized and woven into how individuals with BPD see themselves and their position in the world, societal stigma may translate into self-stigma. Self-stigma is linked with poorer quality of life, self-efficacy, levels of hope, social support, empowerment, and lower functioning in social and professional situations, as well as greater severity of psychiatric symptomatology, according to one study group. Self-stigma is also linked to increased rates of depression, suicidality, and suicide attempts, which is especially concerning for individuals with BPD, whose symptomatology frequently includes suicidal thoughts. Significantly, patients with greater degrees of self-stigma often lose their previous self-concept, according to the researchers, further upsetting an already fragile sense of identity. To put it another way, stigma may exacerbate BPD symptoms.

Within the mental health community, stigma has troubling and harmful consequences. Not only does prejudice towards BPD patients restrict treatment options, but it may also contribute to therapeutic nihilism among clinicians who treat BPD patients, prohibiting providers from working actively toward symptom resolution. Furthermore, unfavorable attitudes about individuals with BPD may reinforce self-stigma, hinder the development of good therapeutic alliances, promote hostile therapy interactions, and lead to discontinuing treatment. BPD symptoms hide patients' humanity, labeling you and serving as your own limits. With such experiences, it is no surprise that individuals with BPD may negatively affect therapy and drop out entirely.

7.6 Breaking Through Prejudice to Find Healing

The elimination of the stigma associated with a borderline personality disorder is obvious and significant. However, as medical understanding and public awareness of BPD increase, advances are being made to break free from prejudice, thanks partly to individuals like Davidson coming up about their experiences with the condition. Of course, eliminating misconceptions about borderline personality disorder takes time; these myths have been around for a long time and run deep. Gaining a better knowledge of the realities of borderline personality disorder, on the other hand, is important to overcoming stigma and assisting individuals in connecting with the therapy they need to recover.

One of the essential things to remember about borderline personality disorder is that it is caused by inner turmoil, which is frequently brought on by traumatic experiences. Experts in BPD now agree that the disorder's symptoms arise as a maladaptive reaction to overwhelming emotions. Even though the thoughts, emotions, and actions that characterize BPD seem illogical, there is the logic behind them. BPD is fundamentally about internal distress that causes immense pain and disturbed responses to that pain. Friends, relatives, and partners of BPD patients may find symptoms difficult to bear, but individuals who suffer from BPD are the ones that feel them the most.

It is also important to remember that BPD isn't a fixed condition. Indeed, most people's symptoms go better with time, according to studies. Instead of being untreatable, individuals with borderline personality disorder seem to be extremely receptive to therapy and obtain substantial, long-lasting symptom alleviation, according to figures.

Part of this treatment's effectiveness may be attributed to the growing availability of effective, high-quality care tailored to individuals with BPD's particular requirements. Most notably, dialectical behavior therapy (DBT), which was developed in the 1980s, has become a cornerstone of BPD treatment. This psychotherapy method is intended to assist patients in creating and receiving acceptance of themselves while generating and receiving meaningful strategies for positive change within the framework of a healthy, compassionate therapeutic partnership. People with BPD may acquire improved emotional control, a more coherent sense of self, and social skills by doing so, without perceiving therapy as rejection and criticism. Connecting with such therapy may be life-changing for individuals with BPD, enabling them to find respite from their disorder's suffering and start a new, more stable, healthier life.

People who have borderline personality disorder are human beings with great worth. You are not defined by your disease, and you do not have to live within the limits of your symptoms. While stigma may create internal and external obstacles to recovery, breaking past stigma to discover effective borderline personality disorder therapy can be transformational, leading to deep healing that will feed and empower you.

Chapter 8: Bonus Meditation

8.1 How to Practice Music Meditation?

Music offers many stress-reducing and general health advantages. It may help you relax your mind without making an effort, which can help you relieve stress. Music may also help you relax by slowing your breathing, lowering the blood pressure, and causing other changes.

Meditation is one of the most effective stress management techniques. For a good reason, it provides immediate advantages such as a quiet mind and body and the ability to develop stress resistance over time. When music and meditation are combined, the beneficial benefits of both are amplified, and you experience more stress reduction.

Music meditation may also seem easier and more immediately calming than other kinds of meditation for many individuals who are new to meditation or who are perfectionists. It is a stress-relieving method that anybody can do. This meditation may help you better manage stress if you practice it on a regular basis.

Time Required

While 20 minutes is a recommended minimum for music therapy, even one song may assist with stress relief and energy restoration.

Instructions for Music Mediation

- Choose music that will help you relax, such as meditation music. This implies choosing music that you like listening to—for example, if you don't like classical music, don't choose it. You should also seek music with a slower pace and, ideally, no words since lyrics may be distracting and involve your conscious mind, which we want to slow down.

- Relax by settling into a comfortable position. Many people believe they must sit with their legs crossed or use a meditation cushion, but the truth is that you should attempt whichever posture seems most comfortable to you. If you are tired, some individuals avoid laying down since they fall asleep faster this way; you may experiment to see what works best for you. Relax your muscles, close your eyes, and breathe via your diaphragm after you have reached a comfortable position. Allow your belly, shoulders, and even facial muscles to relax.

Inhale deeply via your nose, softly extending your abdomen instead of your chest, and then exhale through your mouth.

- Keep your attention on the music. If you find yourself wondering about other things (or even about the music), gradually bring your focus back to the current moment, the music's sound, and the emotions it generates in your body. Make an effort to experience the music.

- Continue doing this for a few minutes or until your timer runs out. As ideas arise, slowly let them go and focus your attention on the music, the current moment, and the bodily sensations you are experiencing. The aim of this exercise is to silence your inner critic and just 'be.' So just 'be' with the music and completely immerse yourself, and you'll find yourself feeling more relaxed in no time.

Tips

- Start with only a few songs and gradually build up to extended practice sessions.

- Switch to a new kind of music if the music is causing you to have a lot of feelings, memories, and internal conversation. Instrumental music, which includes classical, new age, jazz, and other genres, is less distracting than other kinds of music.

- You may schedule your practice according to the number of songs you select, so you don't have to worry about running out of time.

- Don't be too hard on yourself if you find yourself 'thinking too much at first; this is normal for people new to meditation. Instead, pat yourself on the back for recognizing your inner voice and bringing your focus back to the current moment.

8.2 How Mindfulness Meditation Can Help Borderline Personality Disorder

Psychiatrists, psychologists, and other mental health practitioners have increasingly integrated mindfulness meditation practice into their psychotherapy practice during the last decade. Many mental disorders, such as generalized anxiety disorder, chronic pain, major depressive disorder, and borderline personality disorder, may benefit from mindfulness meditation (BPD).

What Is Mindfulness Meditation?

Mindfulness meditation is about being extremely focused and remaining in the present moment without criticizing others.

You practice mindfulness meditation by not thinking about the future or the past and instead focusing on the present now. You practice being aware of what is going on around you, such as various sensations such as smell, see, and touch.

Because mindfulness is about not passing judgment, you should consider these things objectively.

The Buddhist spiritual path has a concept called mindfulness. Buddhist monks have been practicing mindfulness meditation for over 3,000 years. Outside of Buddhism, mindfulness meditation has grown more popular in recent years.

In reality, most Eastern mindfulness practitioners see it as a technique that may be utilized independently of any religious or spiritual practice. Mindfulness meditation may be beneficial for you regardless of your religious background.

What Does Mindfulness Meditation Have to Do with the borderline personality disorder?

One of the first people to use mindfulness meditation practice in the treatment of BPD was Marsha Linehan, Ph.D., the founder of dialectical behavior therapy for BPD. Individuals with BPD often not only feel strong emotions but also get "stuck" in them, judging both the emotions and them.

Unfortunately, this may exacerbate the intensity of the feeling. Judgmental thoughts may contribute to the mix of feelings; for example, if you tell yourself, you are weak for being sad, you could feel both sad and embarrassed.

Individuals with BPD may benefit from mindfulness meditation training to improve their ability to use healthy coping strategies in the face of emotional distress. Mindfulness abilities enable you to create a little amount of space in which you may recognize the feeling and be smarter about how you will respond to it.

Consider getting in a verbal fight with someone you care about. You may experience strong emotions such as rage, fear, and anger during the debate. You are more inclined to act on these emotions if you don't have

mindfulness skills since you cannot see the consequences. You may scream at your partner, hurl something at them, or storm out.

You may be able to recognize your feelings as a result of mindfulness meditation practice, and you may be able to take a step back and choose appropriate action, such as taking a break, unless you can discuss things calmly.

8.3 Religious or Spiritual Meditation

There are many holy texts and religious/spiritual books available. They've all got a lot to say about the human condition. Meditating on what these books say may assist with the most self-destructive aspects of borderline personality disorder, such as poor self-esteem. Many verses from Quran, Bible and other religious books have verses that people use to meditate on. Also, it is believed that these verses help in soothing and providing peace to the heart, reducing depression and promoting hope and will among the people who have tried the religious meditation. These are many instances of such holy texts that are worth good for meditating on. You might be able to come up with your own. It is important to do what's best for you.

Spiritual meditation is a practice that leads you to the roots of who you are. You, as your true self, are devoid of all the notions you have about yourself. In the process, you feel pleasure and serenity. A sense of love and brightness warms up your being.

Spiritual meditation helps you understand the ultimate truth and let go of everything that has occurred and would happen. The present is where you are at, and you should take comfort in it. The desire to practice spiritual meditation arises from an inherent yearning to perceive and think beyond the chaotic environment around you.

1. Find a Relaxing Position

The essential thing to do before you start practicing is to locate a comfortable location and posture. This entails avoiding as much as possible city sounds and surrounding oneself with nature and the calm chirping of birds. Spiritual meditation can send you to sleep fast. To prevent this, you must use great caution while choosing a meditation posture. Choose a posture that is comfortable for you but not one that is too relaxing and will cause you to fall asleep quickly. You may also sit with your back straight on a chair or stand with your back against the wall. Whatever works for you. Then gently shut your eyes.

2. Be a part of the process

What do you typically do when you have a job to complete? You make a strategy, see the process in your mind, and deliberately follow the pattern. We carefully prepare and carry out each one. This, however, is not the best method to approach meditation. You'll have to let it go here. Relax and allow it to run its course in an organic and natural way. You should remain a passive observer, allowing the process to unfold naturally. Do not be worried about the result or about doing it perfectly. Allow things to take their natural course.

3. Recognize Your Thoughts

We live in an information-driven world. You are constantly bombarded with fresh information through breaking news, live updates, and social media. Consequently, your mind is always buzzing with fresh information and the reactions of your brain to it. It is never going to stop when you are awake, and it is much more difficult to quiet your racing thoughts while you are sleeping.

Every idea makes you respond, and you end up being influenced by it. Thoughts will assault you even as you sit to meditate. However, the difficulty comes in refusing to react to them and enabling them to dominate you. Allow ideas and feelings to come to you naturally, but resist the temptation to respond to them. Allow them to flow.

4. Say a few words of prayer

Choose a prayer in your mind while sitting there, keeping your thoughts from defaming your peaceful demeanor. The prayer does not have to be religious. You are free to say anything that is beneficial to you or that you like. It may be a single word or a sentence. If you are a nature enthusiast, it might be anything connected to wildlife or something that makes you joyful. It is perhaps possible that it is a mantra.

Maintain a loose and relaxed body now. Breathe gently and naturally. Observe your breath when it enters your body and when it leaves. Thoughts may hinder your meditation. After each mental interruption, return to your body and breathing. Then, when you exhale, recall your prayer. Then every time that you exhale, repeat the prayer in your mind. Make use of it to return your focus to your breathing.

5. Examine Yourself

Concentrate on your body, as well as your consciousness and presence in the place. Make yourself aware of your surroundings. Take note of how your body feels. Pay attention to your thoughts and breathing. Relax fully and retain your composure. Open your eyes slowly and sit in the same posture for a while. Allow meditation's benefits to settle in. Feel it, and appreciate and understand the sensation of calmness in your body. Consider the whole process and how you did it.

Finally, leave the meditation zone, relax a little, and resume your normal routine.

8.4 Traditional Meditation

The good news is that you don't have to meditate in a challenging yoga position, though poses may be beneficial. Kneeling with hands on your knees is a good position. After that, you can shut your eyes and concentrate on nothingness. This is a really relaxing position, and it is simple to maintain.

You may also concentrate on a mantra, which is a word or phrase that you repeat repeatedly. Because a mantra is such a personal thing, you should pick something that suits your needs or, if you have a teacher, something that he or she suggests. Traditional meditation may benefit from the addition of mantras.

You may discover that whichever form of meditation you select is very helpful to you. Mindfulness meditation, for example, has been proven to alter brain structure and even aid in the treatment of medical ailments. For people with BPD, meditation is a powerful healing tool. You have nothing to lose and everything to gain by giving it a go. Best of luck!

Chapter 9: Some Strategies for Supporting Someone with BPD

If you have a friend or family member who suffers from borderline personality disorder (BPD), you understand how stressful it can be. And you may be stumped as to how you might be of assistance.

Emotional instability, interpersonal problems, and impulsive, sometimes self-destructive behaviors are all symptoms of borderline personality disorder (BPD). BPD patients have strong emotions and often mistrust themselves and others, making relationships challenging for all parties involved.

An unstable or fragmented sense of self is thought to be the fundamental cause of BPD. This is often, but not always, linked to abandonment or early childhood trauma. Not everyone who is traumatized as a kid develops BPD, implying that BPD, like other mental illnesses, is caused by a mix of psychological, biological, and social variables.

Relationships are difficult and demanding because of BPD's nature. Families and friends of people diagnosed with BPD often have concerns about how to assist them.

Support networks may be helpful in assisting a person with BPD in managing and reducing troublesome symptoms.

The following methods listed below may assist you in supporting someone with BPD:

9.1. Learn about BPD.

Normal everyday frustrations, for example, are often transformed into severe interpersonal problems in people with BPD. However, depending on how others respond, these disputes may be minimized or avoided. Most individuals, for example, will take a canceled lunch date in stride and just rearrange their calendar. A canceled lunch, on the other hand, is more likely to be perceived as rejection or abandonment by someone with BPD, resulting in a strong emotional response. Rather than just changing their plans and rescheduling, someone with BPD may get enraged and agitated, rejecting further interaction or demanding urgent contact.

Recognize this reaction as a fear-based misunderstanding and express your desire to connect as a constructive response. Instead of responding to unpleasant or improper behavior, focus on rescheduling the date.

9.2. Show confidence and respect.

There is a strong link between BPD and early childhood trauma. Trauma in early infancy reduces a person's feeling of safety and control over themselves, others, and the environment. Support persons should approach the connection with a person with BPD in a manner that fosters respect and trust, which may be beneficial and therapeutic. Allow the person with BPD to make their own choices, even if you believe you know what is best for them. Demonstrate your faith in their skills and inquire about how you can assist.

9.3. Be trustworthy.

Many individuals with borderline personality disorder have a history of attachment issues, which causes them to be fearful and distrustful of others. It is critical for you to be constant and truthful as a support person. Do what you claim you'll do as much as possible. Setting boundaries ahead of time is acceptable and often essential. Concentrate on what you have to give in terms of time and money.

9.4 Manage conflict with attachment.

Attachment is about long-term caring and sharing good and terrible moments together. Conflicts and arguments are challenging for individuals with BPD because they perceive them as signs of indifference or the end of a relationship, leading to emotions of rage and shame.

Support persons may assist the person with BPD gain perspective and see disagreement as a normal component of a healthy relationship. There is a feeling of acceptance and connection that may heal and produce real change in BPD when a support person remains involved despite challenges.

After a disagreement, support persons may assist by phoning or visiting. Focus on the person rather than the behavior and show compassion and forgiveness. You may accept the person while rejecting the behavior. BPD sufferers need to know that you aren't giving upon them.

9.5 Encourage Professional Help.

Some of the most challenging symptoms of BPD, such as interpersonal difficulties and self-harming behaviors, have been found to improve with individual and group treatment. Other mental illnesses that need therapy, such as anxiety and depression, maybe assessed by mental health experts. Support staff may offer information and, if necessary, help with scheduling appointments. Knowing that assistance is accessible may give individuals with BPD hope.

9.6. Identify strengths.

BPD may be thought of as an issue with self-identity. People with BPD are insecure about themselves and how others see them. Everyone has their own set of skills and talents. People who provide support may assist by highlighting good traits and particular skills that they have seen. It is critical that you be truthful and can provide examples of when the individual exhibited these characteristics. Make a note of good efforts to cope and behavioral improvements.

9.7. Have fun together.

When individuals share pleasant feelings and feel good together, healthy relationships and bonds develop. Suggestion of a healthy, mutually pleasant activity, such as a stroll in nature, attending a concert, gardening, or seeing a funny movie, is one of the most beneficial and therapeutic things a support person can do. Together, these self-soothing activities help both the person with the disorder and the support person while also establishing a healthy connection.

9.8. Take suicide seriously.

Suicide is more common in people with BPD than in the general population. Whether someone speaks about taking their life or makes suicide gestures, it is essential to find out if they are serious about it. Tell the individual that you will take action if you are worried about their safety because you care. If you are not sure what to do, call a crisis line or look into local mental health resources.

Chapter 10: Splitting in Borderline Personality Disorder

The way we think, feel, and act defines our personalities. Our environment, experiences, and inherited characteristics all influence them. Our personalities play an important role in distinguishing ourselves from others around us.

Personality disorders are mental illnesses that lead you to think, feel, and act in ways that are different from the norm. They may create discomfort or difficulties in the lives of those who have them if they are not addressed.

A borderline personality disorder is a fairly prevalent personality condition (BPD). It is characterized by the following characteristics

- problems with one's own image

- trouble controlling emotions and conduct

- Relationships that are insecure

Splitting countertransference, or simply "splitting," is a common tendency among people with BPD.

10.1 What is splitting in BPD?

To divide something is to separate it. People with BPD have a tendency to categorize themselves, others, and events in black-and-white terms. In other words, they may categorize people, things, ideas, or circumstances as all good or all evil in an instant.

They may do so despite knowing that the world is complicated and that good and evil may coexist in the same space.

BPD sufferers often seek external affirmation without taking into account their own feelings about themselves, people, things, beliefs, and circumstances. As a result of the anxiety created by the possibility of desertion, loss of trust, and betrayal, they may be more prone to splitting.

10.2 How long does splitting last?

BPD patients often have strong concerns of abandonment and instability. They may utilize splitting as a defensive strategy to deal with their concerns. This implies they may be able to distinguish between good and negative emotions about:

- objects
- themselves
- beliefs
- situations
- other people

Splitting often happens in a cyclical and abrupt manner. A person with BPD is able to perceive the world in all of its aspects. They do, however, often change their emotions from good to negative.

Before changing, a splitting event may continue for days, months, weeks, or even years.

10.3 What can cause a splitting episode?

An incident that leads a person with BPD to adopt extreme emotional views usually triggers a split. These occurrences may be ordinary, such as needing to travel for work or getting into a fight with someone.

Minor distinctions from someone they care about are often triggering events that cause fear of abandonment.

10.4 Examples of splitting

The vocabulary of a person with BPD is the most frequent way to detect splitting. They often utilize exaggerated terms to describe themselves, people, things, beliefs, and circumstances, such as:

- "bad" and "good"
- "none" and "all"
- "never" and "always"

Here are some examples:

Example 1

In general, you have been feeling good about yourself. You are on a road trip one day when you take a wrong turn and get momentarily confused. Suddenly, whatever positive emotions you had about yourself vanish, and you become very depressed.

You may tell yourself or others negative things such as, "I'm such an idiot, I constantly get lost" or "I'm so useless, I cannot do anything properly."

Making a mistake turn when driving does not, however, imply that a person is useless. However, if a person with BPD does the work first, they may divide their perspective to escape the worry of others thinking they are useless.

Example 2

You have a mentor whom you admire much. You learn to idealize them since they have helped you personally and professionally. If they are so successful in both their personal and professional life, they must be flawless. You tell them that you want to be like them.

Then, one day, your mentor's marriage becomes turbulent. This is seen as a show of weakness by you. Suddenly, your mentor seems to be a total fake and failure to you.

You don't want to have anything to do with them. You distance yourself and your work from them entirely, and you seek a new mentor somewhere.

The abrupt change in your perspective may cause the individual to feel wounded, irritated, and puzzled.

10.5 How does splitting affect relationships?

Splitting is an unintentional effort to protect one's ego and avoid distress. Splitting up leads to intense — and often harmful — behavior in relationships, as well as psychological turmoil. Those attempting to assist individuals with BPD are often confused by splitting.

Splitting is an unintentional effort to protect one's ego and avoid distress.

BPD patients often describe having passionate and insecure relationships. Someone who is seen as a friend one day may be regarded as an enemy the next. A person with BPD may exhibit the following relationship characteristics:

- Trouble trusting people, unreasonably fearful of others' intentions, and rapidly breaking off contact with someone they believe would leave them

- Feelings for a person change quickly, ranging from great intimacy and affection (idealization) to extreme hate and anger (devaluation)

- forming physical and emotional close connections quickly

10.6 What's the best way to cope with splitting if you have BPD?

Splitting is a typical defensive strategy developed by individuals who have been subjected to early life traumas such as abuse or abandonment.

Long-term therapy includes developing coping strategies that help you get a better understanding of the events in your life. Anxiety reduction may also help.

Here's what you can do if you are having trouble coping with a splitting episode right now:

- Breathe slowly and deeply. A rush of anxiousness often come with splitting episodes. Taking deep, long breaths may help you relax and keep your strong emotions at bay.

- Concentrate on all of your senses. Grounding yourself in what is going on around you at any particular time may be a useful approach to distract yourself from strong emotions and help you put things into perspective. In a single instant, what can you taste, hear, smell, touch, and see?

- Make contact. Consider seeking help from a mental health expert if you feel yourself separating.

They may be able to help you relax and cope with the breakup while it is occurring.

10.7 What's the best way to help a person who's experiencing splitting?

It is difficult to assist someone with BPD who is experiencing splitting. You may feel helpless in the face of their symptoms. Here are some suggestions if you feel qualified to assist:

- You should be aware of your loved one's triggers. The repetition of the same experiences is a common BPD trigger. Understanding what triggers your loved one, warning them, and assisting them in avoiding or coping with those triggers may help you avoid or deal with a splitting cycle.

- Recognize your own limitations. Be honest if you don't feel prepared to assist your loved one deal with their BPD splitting episodes. Inform them of when they should seek expert assistance. Here's how to receive treatment on a shoestring budget.

Chapter 11: Treatments and Therapies

Borderline personality disorder has a bad reputation for being difficult to treat. However, many individuals with the condition report fewer or milder symptoms and a better quality of life, thanks to modern, evidence-based treatments. Evidence-based, customized therapy from a properly qualified practitioner is critical for individuals with a borderline personality disorder. Other kinds of therapy and treatment given by a therapist or doctor who is not properly trained may not be beneficial to the individual.

Many variables influence how quickly symptoms improve once therapy starts, so individuals with borderline personality disorder and their loved ones must be patient and receive adequate support during treatment.

11.1 Goals of treatment

The following are essential objectives for many individuals with BPD: to overcome emotional difficulties (such as sadness, anxiety, and rage) and to have a greater sense of purpose in life (e.g., by a positive contribution)

- To improve interpersonal connections

- To develop self-awareness and the ability to live with oneself

- To improve one's physical condition

11.2 When should treatment start?

People with BPD should seek therapy as soon as possible. It is critical to obtain a diagnosis as soon as possible so that a medical expert (such as your psychiatrist, GP, or clinical psychologist) can put together the best treatment plan for you.

You may begin therapy even if your diagnosis isn't clear. Many of the psychological therapies that work for BPD may also help people with other mental illnesses.

BPD may affect young individuals, including teenagers, and therapy can begin as soon as the diagnosis is established.

11.3 Tests and Diagnosis

A certified mental health practitioner with expertise diagnosing and treating mental illnesses, such as a psychologist, psychiatrist, or clinical social worker, may diagnose borderline personality disorder by:

- Completing a comprehensive interview, which includes a discussion of symptoms

- Conducting a comprehensive medical examination that may help rule out other potential causes of symptoms

- Inquiring about medical histories in the family, especially any history of mental illness

Other mental disorders often coexist with a borderline personality disorder. Borderline personality disorder may be difficult to identify and treat due to co-occurring disorders, particularly if symptoms of other diseases coincide with those of borderline personality disorder. A person with BPD, for example, is more prone to suffer from depression, bipolar illness, anxiety disorders, drug abuse disorders, and eating disorders.

11.4 One major challenge: finding effective treatment

Despite the reasons for optimism, effective treatments for BPD sufferers and their loved ones are often difficult to find and obtain. Despite the fact that DBT has been around since the early 1990s, there are few DBT programs in British Columbia.

Nonetheless, there have been some encouraging developments across the province. The Dialectical Behavior Therapy Centre of Vancouver, as well as the formation of DBT-oriented services at Tri-Cities Mental Health, Vancouver General Hospital, and Surrey Memorial Hospital, are among these. DBT training has been provided to a child and youth mental health professionals throughout the province by the Ministry of Children and Family Development. DBT methods are also used in the therapy offered by Correctional Services Canada.

Although progress is being made, many people with BPD continue to suffer and are unable to find adequate help. I'm hoping that this issue of Visions will draw attention to some of the current options for individuals with BPD and raise awareness about the need for more readily available, accessible services for people with BPD. This is a serious issue that must be addressed.

11.5 Seek and Stick with Treatment

According to research sponsored by the National Institute of Mental Health, individuals with borderline personality disorder who do not get appropriate treatment are:

- Other chronic medical or mental disorders are more prone to emerge.

- Less likely to adopt a healthy lifestyle

In comparison to the general population, borderline personality disorder is linked to a substantially greater incidence of self-harm and suicide conduct.

Individuals with this disorder who are considering self-harm or suicide need to get treatment immediately away.

Call the toll-free National Suicide Prevention Lifeline (NSPL) 24 hours a day, seven days a week at 1-800-273-TALK (8255) if you or someone you know is in distress. Everyone is welcome to use the service. The Lifeline may be reached through TTY at 1-800-799-4889 for the deaf and hard of hearing. All calls are completely free and private. If you are worried about a friend's social media posts, contact the social media site immediately, or call 911 in an emergency. Visit the NIMH's Suicide Prevention health issue page to learn more.

The treatments listed on this page are only a few of the options that a person with a borderline personality disorder may have.

11.6 Care program approach (CPA)

If the symptoms you recognize are moderate to severe, you'll most likely be sent to a care program approach for treatment (CPA).

CPA is basically a method of ensuring that you get the best care possible for your specific situation. There are four phases to the process:

- an evaluation of your health and social requirements

- a care plan - tailored to your health and social requirements

- designate a care coordinator (keyworker) – typically a social worker or nurse who will be your initial point of contact with other CMHT members

- Reviews - when your treatment is evaluated on a regular basis, and any required modifications to your care plan are discussed.

11.7 Psychotherapy

For individuals with borderline personality disorder, psychotherapy is the primary line of treatment. A therapist may offer one-on-one therapy with a patient or group treatment. People with borderline personality disorder may benefit from therapist-led group sessions to learn how to connect with others and express themselves effectively.

It is critical for individuals in treatment to like and trust their therapist. People with borderline personality disorder may find it challenging to establish a comfortable and trustworthy relationship with their therapist due to the disorder's nature.

11.8 Dialectical behavior therapy (DBT)

Dialectical behavior therapy is a kind of treatment that was created specially to help individuals with borderline personality disorder.

Dialectical behavior therapy is founded on the notion that two major factors cause the borderline personality disorder:

- You are very sensitive emotionally – such as, low-stress levels make you feel highly worried.

- You raised in an atmosphere where people around you disregarded your emotions — for example, if you complained of worry or tension, a parent might have warned you that you had no right to be unhappy or that you were simply "being stupid."

These two elements may lead to a vicious cycle in which you experience strong and unpleasant emotions while also feeling worthless and guilty for experiencing them. You believe that experiencing these feelings makes you a terrible person because of your background. These feelings are then amplified by these ideas.

DBT aims to interrupt the pattern by teaching two key concepts:

- Accepting that your feelings are genuine, authentic, and acceptable.

- Dialectics is a philosophical system that holds that most things in life are seldom "black and white" and that it is essential to be open to opposing ideas and viewpoints.

The DBT therapist will use both ideas in order to help you make good behavioral adjustments.

For example, the therapist may accept (validate) that your self-harm as a result of deep sorrow and that your behavior does not make you a horrible and useless person.

The therapist would next attempt to counter the notion that self-harm is the only way to deal with sorrow.

DBT's ultimate aim is to help you "break free" from a limited, inflexible way of viewing the world, your relationships, and your life that leads to self-destructive and harmful behavior.

Weekly individual and group sessions are typically part of DBT, and you'll be given an out-of-hours phone number to call if your symptoms worsen.

DBT is a team-based therapy. You'll be required to collaborate with your therapist and other group members. As a result, the therapists collaborate as a team.

Women with Borderline personality disorder who have a history of suicidal and self-harming behavior have found DBT especially helpful. The National Institute for Health and Care Excellence (NICE) recommends it as the initial therapy for these women.

11.9 Mentalization-based therapy (MBT)

Mentalization-based treatment is another form of long-term psychotherapy that may be used to treat borderline personality disorder.

MBT is founded on the idea that individuals with BPD have a limited mental capacity.

The capacity to think about thinking is known as mentalization. This entails evaluating your own ideas and views to see whether they are helpful, practical, and grounded in reality.

Many individuals with BPD, for example, may have a sudden desire to self-harm and then act on it without thought. They lack the capacity to "take a step back" and tell themselves, "That's not a healthy way of thinking, and I'm only going to think this way because I'm angry."

Another essential aspect of mentalization is to understand that other people have their own ideas, feelings, beliefs, desires, and needs and that your perception of their mental states may not always be accurate. Furthermore, you must be mindful of the possible effect of your activities on the mental states of others.

The aim of MBT is to increase your capability to comprehend your own and others' mental states and learn to "stand back" from and analyze your own and others' ideas.

MBT may be administered in a hospital setting, where you will be admitted as an inpatient. Daily individual appointments with group sessions or therapists with other individuals with BPD are typically part of the therapy.

A typical MBT course lasts around 18 months. During this period, several hospitals and specialized centers urge you to stay in the hospital as an inpatient. Other hospitals and centers may advise you to leave the hospital after a specific amount of time but continue to be treated as an outpatient, meaning you return to the hospital on a regular basis.

11.10 Therapeutic communities (TCs)

Therapeutic communities (TCs) are organized settings in which individuals with a variety of complicated psychological disorders and requirements may connect and participate in treatment.

TCS is intended to assist individuals with long-term emotional issues and a previous history of self-harming by training them on how to engage socially.

The majority of TCs are domestic, such as big homes where you stay for 1 to 4 days each week.

You will be required to participate in additional activities aimed at improving your self-confidence and social skills in addition to individual and group treatment, such as:

- tasks around the home

- preparing the dinner

- sports, games, and other recreational activities

- community gatherings on a regular basis - when residents address any problems that have developed in the neighborhood

The majority of TCs are democratically governed. This implies that each staff member and resident have a say in how the TC is managed, including whether or not a person is eligible to live there.

Even if your care team believes you might benefit from spending some time in a TC, this is no guarantee that the TC will accept you.

Many TCs have rules on what is and aren't appropriate behavior in the community, such as no drinking, no violence towards other residents or employees, and no self-harming efforts. Those who violate these rules are often asked to leave the TC.

While some individuals with BPD have claimed that their symptoms improved after spending time in a TC, there isn't enough data to say if TCs would benefit everyone with BPD.

A TC would also be unsuitable if a person was having considerable difficulty regulating their behavior due to the frequently severe restrictions on behavior.

11.11 Cognitive Behavioral Therapy (CBT)

CBT, known as cognitive-behavioral therapy, is a form of treatment that focuses on both the "cognitive" (thinking-related) and the "behavioral" (action-related) components of a mental health disorder.

CBT is primarily concerned with the present, which means that you spend relatively little time discussing your history. In addition to discussing how you began to learn or behave the way you do; your therapist will likely ask you questions about how your present ways of thinking or behaving are linked to your symptoms and how you might alter these patterns.

The directed nature of CBT means that your therapist will often take an active part in your treatment session, providing you with direct counsel and direction on a regular basis.

While the fundamental concepts of cognitive-behavioral therapy (CBT) may be beneficial for individuals suffering from a borderline personality disorder (BPD), some experts believe that the condition necessitates the use of more specific CBT methods.

Schema-focused therapy

A cognitive-behavioral treatment method based on the principles of cognitive-behavioral therapy and then extended to incorporate techniques and ideas from other psychotherapies, Schema Focused Therapy (SFT) has become more popular. Schema therapists assist patients in altering their self-defeating, entrenched life patterns – or schemas – via the use of cognitive, behavioral, and emotion-focused therapeutic methods. The treatment of borderline personality disorder focuses on the patient's connection with the therapist, everyday life outside of treatment, and the traumatic childhood events prevalent in the condition. Participants in the initial trial of SFT for borderline personality disorder were treated for a total of three years in the program.

11.12 Transference-Focused Therapy (TFT)

In the treatment of borderline personality disorder (BPD), transference-focused therapy (TFT) is a kind of psychotherapy that focuses on changing the way you interact to other people in the world via your therapeutic relationship with your therapist. This may assist you in identifying troubling thoughts, developing better habits, and improving social relationships, among other things.

According to the theory behind these kinds of treatments, the therapist will be able to read your thoughts and emotions about significant individuals in your life, such as your parents or siblings. You then begin to feel and respond toward the therapist in the same way as you would toward these significant people in your life.

Through transference, it is hoped that the therapist will be able to observe your interactions with other people and utilize this knowledge to assist you in developing more healthy connections.

Therapists who specialize in transference-focused treatment for borderline personality disorder (BPD) think that the primary etiology of BPD is linked to dysfunctional connections in childhood that continue to have an effect on teenage and adult relationships. Your sense of self and mental representations of others are said to be formed via your interactions with our caregivers throughout early infancy, according to the idea. If anything goes wrong during this process, individuals may have trouble developing a strong sense of self or experiencing difficulties in their relationships with other people.

A growing body of research suggests that early maltreatment or the loss of primary caregivers during childhood increases the risk of developing BPD, and because the symptoms of BPD include significant difficulties in interpersonal relationships and an unstable sense of one's own identity, some experts have proposed that BPD should be treated by establishing better relationships by the use of transference.

People who are participating in TFP meet with their therapist twice a week. Throughout these sessions, the therapist will use methods from the field of object relations. The significance of social contact in helping individuals alter their maladaptive habits is emphasized by object relations theory. These methods may include the following:

- Developing a relationship of trust between the individual and the therapist

- Creating limits that are related to the individual's particular symptoms is important.

- The study of behavior patterns, emotions, and one's sense of self, and how these aspects affect one's capacity to deal with adversity

- Increasing awareness of potentially harmful or hazardous actions

- Learning to change emotional states and enhance relationships may aid in the relief of symptomatic conditions.

11.13 Arts therapies

Individual or group arts or creative treatments may be provided as part of a therapy program for individuals with BPD.

Therapies may include:

- dance movement therapy

- art therapy

- music therapy

- drama therapy

Arts therapy is intended to assist individuals who have difficulty verbally expressing their ideas and emotions. The emphasis of the treatment is on producing something as a means of expressing your emotions.

The classes are led by licensed therapists who can assist you in considering what you have produced and how it connects to your own ideas and experiences.

Weekly sessions of up to 2 hours are typically part of an art therapy program.

11.14 Treating a crisis

If you believe you are in a crisis, you will most likely be given numerous phone numbers to call (when you have an increased risk of self-harm, and the symptoms are severe).

Your community mental health nurse is likely to be one of these numbers. Other numbers you may need include a social worker's after-hours phone number and the number for your local crisis resolution team (CRT).

Crisis resolution teams help individuals with significant mental illnesses who are in the midst of an acute or severe psychiatric crisis that would need hospitalization if not for the intervention of the team. A Suicide attempt is an indication of a serious mental crisis.

People with BPD often discover that just talking to someone who knows their illness may help them get out of a bad situation.

In a limited number of instances, you may be prescribed a brief course of medication to help you relax, such as a tranquilizer. This medication is typically given for a period of seven days.

If your symptoms are extremely severe and it is determined that you are a substantial danger to your own health, you may be sent to hospital – or, in rare cases, detained under the Mental Health Act if you are unable to make appropriate safety choices. This will only be for a short while, and you should be able to go home after your symptoms have improved. Doctors try to avoid keeping patients unless it is absolutely necessary.

11.15 Hospitalization

If the symptoms are severe, your therapist or doctor may suggest that you seek care in a hospital. You may also be admitted to the hospital if you engage in suicidal conduct, have suicidal thoughts, or are considering hurting yourself or others.

11.16 Medications

Experts are split on whether medication is beneficial. There is presently no medication approved to treat BPD.

While the National Institute for Health and Care Excellence (NICE) does not promote medication, there is evidence that it may assist certain individuals with specific conditions.

Medication is seldom used as the main therapy for borderline personality disorder since the advantages are uncertain. A psychiatrist may, however, prescribe medicines to address particular symptoms such as:

- depression
- mood swings
- other co-occurring mental disorders

Medication treatment may need the assistance of several medical professionals.

The following are some of the most frequently recommended medicines for BPD:

- Antidepressants - these may assist those who are depressed or anxious.

- Antipsychotics were among the first medicines used to treat BPD. They may be especially beneficial for some of the more troublesome symptoms of the disorder, such as rage, impulsivity, and fearful thinking.

- Anxiolytics (anti-anxiety medicines) - Because anxiety and BPD are often linked, some of the medicines may be beneficial. However, some of these medications can be addictive, making them a double-edged blade.

- Anticonvulsants and mood stabilizers - Mood stabilizers and anticonvulsants may assist with impulsivity and emotional reactivity.

Other therapies, such as omega-3 fatty acids, are being researched as well. Second-generation antipsychotics and mood stabilizers provide the strongest indication for medication benefit in BPD.

11.17 Alternative therapy

In individuals with BPD, omega-3 fatty acids may help to alleviate symptoms of sadness and aggressiveness. More study is required to establish omega-3 fatty acid's advantages.

11.18 Tips for Getting the Most Out of BPD Treatment

Participate in your treatment plan.

Treatment for borderline personality disorder is necessary, and you should strive to be an active, involved participant in whatever program you are enrolled in. You'll feel more empowered to ask pertinent questions, offer recommendations, and be open and honest with treatment professionals as you gain more knowledge. There is no one-size-fits-all therapy for BPD. Getting it right may take some time.

Have an emergency plan in place.

The emotional anguish you feel as a result of BPD may be one of the most difficult aspects of the disorder. This may result in a mental health emergency. You may, for example, experience suicidal thoughts or actions. Create an emergency safety plan while you are clear-headed and in a good mood. Make a plan for what you'll do if you think you are a danger to yourself or others.

Create a precise strategy since you may not think as clearly while you are in the middle of a potentially dangerous scenario as you did when you made the plan.

11.19 Overcoming BPD Without Medication

It is possible to overcome BPD without medication, but you should always follow your doctor's or health care provider's advice and treatment plan. In most instances, medication isn't the first line of defense against BPD. It is usually reserved for the treatment of particular symptoms like depression or mood swings.

Whether or whether you take medicine for BPD, you may develop coping skills and live a healthy lifestyle without allowing the disease and its symptoms to define you.

It is critical to develop methods that work for you and to change your mindset from one of negativity to one of positivity. You may also wish to open out about your requirements to family and friends. Assist loved ones in recognizing and understanding how to help you when you are angry or upset, for example. Loved ones are likely to want to assist and support you but may not know-how.

Chapter 12: Other Elements of Care

Some individuals with borderline personality disorder have severe symptoms and need inpatient or intensive treatment. Others may need some outpatient procedures **for treatment** but never need to be admitted to the hospital or get emergency care.

12.1 How to try to keep anxiety down at all times

Emotional highs and lows, impulsive conduct, and sensitivity are all common symptoms of borderline personality disorder (BPD). Many individuals with BPD suffer from severe emotional instability or significant swings between feeling good and sad or depressed. In response to certain situations, such as a dispute with a friend, you may find that your emotions shift rapidly.

Often, your emotional responses are out of proportion to the event that causes them, such as feeling so unhappy that you start crying over a little inconvenience.

People with BPD often experience emotions far more strongly than others, and those sensations may take longer to dissipate. This implies that circumstances or occurrences that would not bother a normal person may be very distressing and disturbing to someone with BPD.

Other symptoms of this disease, such as impulsivity, may also be caused by this underlying instability. All of this may cause chaos in your relationships, job, mood, and general functioning.

While certain medicines may assist with emotional instability, you can also adopt lifestyle modifications to help significantly decrease this condition.

This may include avoiding certain harmful coping strategies in the past and instead of using skills to assist you self-regulate. Making these adjustments may help you better control your emotional reactions and decrease the frequency and severity of your emotions.

Before beginning any treatment policy to tackle emotional instability, speak with your therapist about your concerns to ensure that you don't compromise your therapy. They may even assist you in managing your emotions as a result of these changes.

Get Quality Sleep

Have you ever observed that when you are sleepy, you are more prone to being upset by little irritations? Sleep deprivation may alter how you see and react to your environment. In fact, lack of sleep may lead individuals to respond adversely to situations that they would normally consider neutral.

One of the essential things you can do to decrease your emotional instability and irritation is to get a decent night's sleep.

What does it mean to get a "good night's sleep"? While the answer varies from person to person, most people should aim for between 7 and 9 hours of sleep each night.

If you have difficulty falling or staying asleep, you may enhance your sleep in general and help you get through your weekdays with less emotional anguish by doing the following:

Maintaining a consistent schedule.

Before going to bed, stay away from alcohol and caffeine.

Keeping your space at a suitable temperature (and cool).

At least an hour before night, turn off all lights and gadgets.

Exercise

It is no secret that exercising your body makes you feel better physically and psychologically. Exercise not only helps to combat a variety of physical health issues connected with BPD, but it also helps to maintain a more stable emotional system. If you don't already have an exercise routine, talk to your doctor about which kind of exercise is best for you. Then you may start your own workout program by following these steps:

- Start simple, and don't push yourself too much. If you are eager to get started, you may force yourself too hard and injure yourself. Instead, over time, gradually increase the duration and intensity of your exercises.

- Experiment with various kinds of workouts. Trying out a range of workouts may help you figure out which kind you like, making it more likely that you'll stay with it. You may like solo exercises, or you might want something more team-oriented to keep you engaged.

- Incorporate stress-relieving exercises into your daily routine. Consider soothing types of exercise like tai chi or yoga in addition to weight training and cardio. These exercises mix movement with regulated breathing and may aid in stress reduction.

Eat Healthy

When you are feeling down, you are more inclined to neglect your nutrition. Negative emotions may trigger cravings for unhealthy foods, binge eating, or skipping meals entirely. You may resort to comfort foods to help you cope with stress or sadness. Unfortunately, this may become a vicious cycle since poor nutrition has an adverse effect on mood, making you feel even worse.

Maintaining a nutritious diet, on the other hand, may help you feel better by ensuring you receive the nutrients you need for mental health (your results can vary as it depends on the diet).

If you are unsure where to start, talk to your doctor about creating a strategy that works for you.

Practice Self-Care

Committing to take excellent care of yourself is the greatest approach to minimize emotional ups and downs. With all of your responsibilities, this may be easier said than done, but it is worth the effort to include self-care into your daily routine.

This may include everything that makes you feel satisfied and cared for, such as spending time with friends and family.

Participating in intellectually stimulating or enjoyable activities

Participating in religious or spiritual activities if they are appropriate for your lifestyle.

Relaxation or meditation may help you manage your stress.

Taking care of your entire health by eating properly, getting enough sleep, and exercising

If you can improve your mental well-being, the time you invest in a self-care program will pay you. Self-care may help you manage your symptoms by taking time for yourself, resting, meditating, or even indulging yourself.

Create Structure

When do you notice yourself going through times of emotional turmoil? If you are more prone to experience them when you haven't scheduled anything else to do, establishing a routine may help you remain busy and emotionally stable.

Having a regular daily routine allows you to know what to anticipate, which may help you feel more prepared for each day and more secure in general. Following a

schedule may also help you make time for other healthy activities like exercising, practicing self-care, and cooking nutritious meals.

Practice Mindfulness

During times of emotional turmoil, mindfulness may help you redirect your attention. Mindfulness entails being more aware of yourself and your environment, as well as encouraging you to live in the present moment without judgment.

Living consciously entails being aware of the sights, sounds, and scents around you, as well as your own internal feelings. By deliberately tuned in to those things at any moment throughout the day, you may practice mindfulness. You may give it a shot by:

- Observing the flavors and textures of the food while you are eating

- During a shower, paying attention to the sensation of warm water on your body

- Taking note of the warmth and feel of a hot cup of coffee

- During yoga practice, pay attention to how your body feels.

- Mindfulness may assist with anxiety and stress management.

- Consider taking a mindfulness break if you feel yourself responding emotionally to something that occurred in the past or something that may happen in the future. This exercise may assist you in returning to the present moment.

12.2 Therapy for Caregivers and Family Members

Therapy may also help families and friends of individuals with a borderline personality disorder. It may be difficult to have a family member or loved one with the condition, and family members or caregivers may inadvertently behave in ways that exacerbate their loved one's symptoms.

- Family members, care takers, or loved ones may be included in certain borderline personality disorder treatments. Allowing the family or loved one to acquire skills to better understand and assist a person with a borderline personality disorder is one of the benefits of this kind of treatment.

- Focusing on family members' needs in order to assist them to comprehend the challenges and solutions for caring for somebody with a borderline personality disorder. Although additional study is required to establish the efficacy of family therapy in the treatment of borderline personality disorder, research on other mental illnesses indicates that involving family members in a person's treatment may be beneficial.

12.3 Tips for Family and Caregivers

To assist a friend or family who is suffering from the disorder:

- Provide emotional support, compassion, tolerance, and encouragement—change may be difficult and scary for individuals with borderline personality disorder, but it can improve with time.

- Learn about mental illnesses, such as borderline personality disorder, so you can comprehend what the person suffering from it is going through.

- Encourage your loved one in borderline personality disorder treatment to inquire about family therapy.

- Seek professional help from a therapist. Your loved one with borderline personality disorder should not be attending the same therapist.

12.4 Coping Skills for Borderline Personality Disorder

Your emotions may be overpowering if you have borderline personality disorder (BPD). Unpredictable mood swings, self-harming activities, suicidality, strong emotional experiences, sensitivity to issues in your relationships, and impulsive behavior problems are all symptoms of BPD. These signs and symptoms may all be linked to one thing: emotion dysregulation.

You may have extremely powerful emotional reactions and trouble regulating them if you have emotion dysregulation. Unfortunately, many individuals with BPD resort to harmful behaviors like aggression, self-harm, or drug misuse to deal with their emotional anguish. Emotion dysregulation and other BPD symptoms may be reduced with coping skills.

Benefits of Coping Skills

Many BPD therapies stress the need to develop coping skills to better regulate emotions as they occur since emotion dysregulation is such a prominent characteristic of BPD. What are coping skills, exactly? They are more healthy approaches to dealing with circumstances and the emotions that arise as a consequence of them.

- Learning new coping mechanisms has the potential to be beneficial. These methods may help you: Gain confidence in your abilities to deal with challenging circumstances.

- Improve your capacity to continue to operate normally, even when faced with adversity.

- Reduce the severity of your emotional discomfort.

- Reduce the chance of you doing anything harmful (e.g., self-harming) in an effort to cope with your emotional discomfort.

- When you are angry, you should reduce the chances of engaging in relationship-destroying behaviors (e.g., physical violence).

- In the end, you'll be able to decrease your overall experience of emotion dysregulation.

People employ hundreds of different coping strategies to deal with stressful circumstances and the emotions that accompany them. Here are a few different kinds of coping techniques that many individuals find useful.

Play Music

Play music that makes you feel the opposite of the feeling you are having trouble with. If you are depressed, for example, listen to cheerful, uplifting music. Play calm, soothing music if you are feeling nervous.

Engage in Activity

The term "behavioral activation" is occasionally used to describe this coping technique. Take part in an activity that is both entertaining and educational. Activities like watching television or using a computer do not qualify since they are too passive. Instead, go on a walk, clean your home, dance, or do anything else that will keep you occupied and divert your attention away from your present feelings.

Ride It Out

Most intense emotional responses and desires to participate in harmful behaviors reach a peak for a few minutes before fading. Set a timer for 10 minutes in the kitchen using an egg timer. Allow 10 minutes to pass and try riding out the feeling.

Ground Yourself

Do something to ground yourself when emotions appear to be pulling you out of the present moment, such as when you start to feel "zoned out." To break out from negative thoughts, grab an ice cube and hold it in your palm for a few seconds, or snap a rubber band against your wrist.

Be Mindful

Mindfulness of your emotions is a good thing to do. Notice the feeling you are experiencing and let it wash over you like a wave without attempting to prevent, repress, or hold it back. Accept the feeling for what it is and move on. Try to remain in the present moment so that you don't bring your previous feelings with you.

Pray

Are you a spiritual or religious person? If you attend religious rituals or have contemplated doing so, praying, and visiting weekly congregations may be very beneficial in times of severe stress.

Breathe deeply

One of the most basic relaxing techniques is deep breathing. Sit or lay down someplace quiet and focus on your breathing. Evenly, slowly, and thoroughly breathe. With each breath, notice how your stomach rises and falls. This may help you remain in the current moment.

Take a Bath or Shower in Warm Water

Try to lose yourself in the warm water's sensations or the soap's aroma. Allow the sensations to take your attention away from the issue that is bothering you and concentrate on relaxing your muscles.

Help someone else.

Make a kind gesture for someone else. It doesn't have to be something major; you could just go to the closest shop, purchase a pack of gum, and smile and say "have a nice day" to the cashier. It may seem little, but simple acts like these may help to alleviate mental distress and link you to the outside world.

Find Support

When you are dealing with intense emotions, reaching out to others may be very beneficial. Make a supportive phone call to a friend or family member. If you don't know anybody who can assist you and you are in a crisis, contact a helpline.

12.5 What if the person doesn't want help?

An adult has the right to reject treatment in most cases. However, if their lives are in danger or they cannot agree, they may be treated without their permission.

Tell the individual you are worried, even if the issue isn't an emergency. Make them aware that you are concerned about their ability to get appropriate therapy.

Continue to show your support and acknowledge their viewpoint. Be friendly, open, and nonjudgmental.

Even if they have already committed to their therapy, a person with BPD may refuse to attend their session with their psychiatrist or another therapist. If this occurs, do the following steps:

- Inquire about their concerns and allow them to express themselves.

- Continue to provide emotional support and encouragement to them.

- Discuss what sort of practical assistance they need to continue their therapy.

- For assistance, contact your healthcare provider.

Chapter 13: 7 Stages of Healing of Individuals with Borderline Personality Disorder

Having a personality condition may be disheartening, especially if it is discovered suddenly. BPD has the greatest incidence of awareness of any disorder, and it is even recognized as having the potential to recover completely. There is no other personality condition that can make such a claim.

The reason for this is that people with BPD have a very high degree of emotional awareness and expressiveness, which is extremely visible. Many therapy techniques may effectively focus on the management component due to their capacity to be immediately in touch with their emotional response. In other words, unlike other personality disorders, there is no artificial facade that must be torn down first. You get exactly what you see.

While the tell-tale signs of BPD are easily visible to others, they are not necessarily so to a person suffering from the illness. Most people with BPD learn to accept and wear their individuality with pride after some contemplation and a few steps along the road. Some of those stages are listed below.

13.1 Denial.

All phases of awareness begin with a defensive mechanism, such as denial, and progress from there. Rejecting an issue, problem, death, or divorce is much less difficult than confronting the problem or issue in question. Accepting responsibility for a problem is an important part of admitting one has one. Consequently, a person is forced to admit a series of failed relationships, recurrent disputes, an inability to cope with stress, and some kind of work-related disability throughout their life. In the beginning, denial is a much more convenient reaction.

13.2 Confusion.

Gradually, it becomes hard to overlook one's own life's problems, particularly when one notices that others do not seem to be experiencing the same degree of everyday irritation, conflict, or intensity. This results in the individual seeking assistance to determine what is wrong, which results in the individual being exposed to BPD for the first time. Many people rapidly relapse into dissociation as a form of self-preservation. When confronted with a stressful event, one of the most distinguishing features of a person suffering from BPD is the capacity to go outside of oneself. In many cases, this results in a momentary memory lapse, which only serves to worsen the confusion.

13.3 Resistance.

A person's growing awareness of memory gaps prompts him or her to study more about bipolar disorder. However, there is a significant reluctance to diagnose since another distinguishing feature is impulsivity in potentially hazardous circumstances. Recognizing and taking responsibility for a condition goes hand in hand with acknowledging and accepting responsibility for high-risk conduct. This is unpleasant for anybody, but it may be particularly stressful and distressing for someone suffering from BPD. Instead, it is more convenient to fight the disorder and continue to hold others responsible for the harm.

13.4 Anger.

Persons suffering from BPD experience emotions more strongly than the general population, which is particularly noticeable in their rage outbursts. When they can no longer reject the diagnosis, anger becomes the default emotion, which is often directed towards family members or anybody else who has attempted to assist them along the road. Unfortunately, their reaction causes them to become even more isolated from others, triggering an acute and uncontrolled dread of being abandoned. Others are perplexed by the pushing away with rage followed by the drawing in when they feel abandoned by their partner. As a result, the following phase is triggered.

13.5 Depression.

A person suffering from a borderline personality disorder (BPD) develops a deep sense of loneliness, misunderstanding, and rejection by others. At exactly this point, another hallmark of suicide ideation becomes apparent: despair. Not only is the person suffering from BPD just now starting to understand the enormous disparity between the degrees of strong emotion they possess in contrast to others, but they are also grasping at vastly lost chances and relationships as a result of their condition. The impact of their illness on others has had a devastating effect on them. Everyone's experience with the transition from despair to acceptance is unique and differs. However, depression is needed in order to ignite the desire to go ahead.

13.6 Acceptance.

This is the most favorable of all the phases since they are beginning to open up to the possibility of comprehending the problem at this point. It is no longer seen as a terrible diagnosis but rather as a gift from God. Persons suffering from a borderline personality disorder (BPD) have a rare ability to be aware of not just their own feelings but also the emotions of others. Frequently, they can sense when someone is unhappy before the other person actually knows what is going on. This is very helpful in a variety of professions where it is necessary to correctly understand the emotions of another individual. Acceptance entails learning how to make the most of one's abilities.

13.7 Therapy.

Developing coping strategies for dealing with stress, recognizing the effect of the illness on others, and recovering from a succession of traumatizing experiences are all tasks that must be completed now. This whole cycle is unfortunately often repeated throughout the therapy process as fresh insights are gained and awareness of one's own emotions is acquired. However, after a person has reached the other side of the process, they are able to function normally, and most new acquaintances will have no clue that they are suffering from this illness.

To effectively complete the phases, it will need a great lot of patience on the part of all those who will participate. However, once there, the transformation is breathtakingly dramatic.

Conclusion

BPD is a mental health condition marked by extremes in a person's thinking, feeling, and acting. During periods known as splitting, many individuals with BPD develop exaggerated characterizations about themselves, others, things, beliefs, and circumstances.

Anxiety-related situations often result in splitting episodes. Coping with splitting symptoms is feasible, even though it is tough at times.

Getting expert treatment may help you deal with your BPD and splitting cycles the best way possible. Learning about BPD is the first and the most important step for families, friends, and other support individuals who wish to assist in a meaningful way. When you understand the underlying reason for problematic behavior, you are more likely to react in a helpful way. Learn all you can about borderline personality disorder. It is easy to get offended by someone with BPD's unpredictable conduct. However, the more you learn about the illness and how it affects behavior, the more you'll be able to comprehend your loved one's actions. Recognize your personal boundaries and when the connection is causing you stress. Every relationship has its own set of expectations and involves a certain amount of giving and take. Supporting someone with BPD requires a higher level of commitment than most partnerships. When you need a break, be self-aware and honest with yourself. Consider this a kind of self-care and a healthy connection, rather than criticism and rejection. Your own self-acceptance and self-care provide a strong example for the individual you are helping.

The effect of BPD on the person, their family, and friends may be minimized with regular and appropriate assistance. One of the most beneficial things you can do for someone suffering from BPD is to improve your ability to react in a helpful manner.

Made in the USA
Middletown, DE
30 July 2022

70219685R00116